A Wreath of Stars

A Wreath of Stars

BOB SHAW

DOUBLEDAY & COMPANY, INC.

GARDEN CITY, NEW YORK   1977

All of the characters in the book
are fictitious, and any resemblance
to actual persons, living or dead,
is purely concidental.

ISBN 0-385-12463-5
Library of Congress Catalog Card Number 76–23797
Copyright © 1976 by Bob Shaw
All Rights Reserved
First Edition in the United States of America

A Wreath of Stars

CHAPTER ONE

Gilbert Snook sometimes thought of himself as being the exact social equivalent of a neutrino.

He was an aircraft engineer, and therefore not formally schooled in nuclear physics, but he knew the neutrino to be an elusive particle, one which interacted so faintly with the normal hadronic matter of the universe that it could flit straight through the Earth without hitting or disturbing one other particle. Snook was determined to do much the same thing on his linear course from birth towards death, and—at the age of forty—was well on the way to achieving his aim.

His parents were faded and friendless individuals, with insular tendencies, who had died when he was a child, leaving him little money and no family bonds of any kind. The only type of education made available to Snook by the local authority was of a technical nature, presumably because it was a quick and well-proven way of converting community liabilities into assets, but it had matched his aptitudes quite well. He had worked hard, easily holding his place in the classroom, always leading his group in benchwork. After collecting an adequate sheaf of certificates he had chosen to be an aircraft engineer, mainly because it was a trade which involved extensive foreign travel. He had inherited his parents' liking for solitude and had made full use of his professional mobility to avoid concentrations of people. For almost two decades he had shuttled through the Near and Middle East, impartially selling his skills to anyone—oil company, airline or military organisation—who was straining aircraft to the limits and was prepared to pay well to keep them flying.

Those years had seen the painful splintering of Africa and Arabia into smaller and smaller statelets, and there had been times when he had found himself in danger of becoming associated or identified with one upflung political entity or another. The involvement might have resulted in anything from having to accept a permanent job to facing an executioner's machine gun while it counted its lethal rosary of brass and lead. But in each case—neutrino-like—he had slipped away, unscathed, before the trap of circumstance could close on him. When necessary, he had changed his name for short periods or had accepted different types of work. He had kept moving, and nothing had touched him.

In the microcosms of nuclear physics, the only particle which could threaten the existence of a neutrino would be an anti-neutrino; and it was ironic, therefore, that it was a cloud of those very particles which—in the summer of 1993—interacted so violently with the life of the human neutrino, Gil Snook.

The cloud of anti-neutrinos were first observed crossing the orbit of Jupiter on the third day of January, 1993—and, because of the extreme difficulty of detecting its existence at all, the astronomers were quite content to use the term "cloud" in their early reports. It was not until a month had passed that they dropped the word and inserted in its place the more accurate, though highly emotive, phrase "rogue planet."

This closer definition of the phenomenon was made possible by improvements in the newly invented magniluct viewing equipment, which—as so often has happened in the history of scientific discovery had come along at the precise moment it was required.

Magniluct was a material which looked like ordinary blue glass, but in fact it was a sophisticated form of quantum amplifier which acted like a low-light camera, without the latter's complex electronics. Goggles or glasses with magniluct lenses made it possible to see clearly at night, giving the wearer the impression that his surroundings were illuminated by blue floodlights. Military applications, such as the use of magniluct spectacles in night-fighting, had come first—providing the inventor/manufacturers with handsome dividends —but an astute marketing team had promoted the new material in many other fields. Miners, photographic darkroom staff, speleologists, night watchmen and police, theatre ushers, taxi and train drivers—anybody who had to work in darkness was a prospective customer. Staff in astronomical observatories found magniluct spectacles particularly useful because, thus equipped, they could work efficiently without splashing unwanted light over colleagues and instruments.

Also in the classic tradition of scientific discovery was the circumstance that it was an amateur astronomer, working in a home-made dome in North Carolina, who became the first man to see the rogue planet as it drew nearer to the sun.

Clyde Thornton was a good astronomer, not in the modern usage of the word—which might have implied that he was a competent mathematician or stellar physicist—but good in the sense that he loved looking at the heavens and knew his way around them better than he knew the district of Asheville in which he had grown up. He also could locate every item in his small observation dome in pitch darkness, and therefore had bought his pair of magniluct glasses a week previously as much out of curiosity as for any practical reason. Thornton liked and appreciated technical novelties, and the idea of an inert transparency which turned night into day intrigued him.

He had set up his telescope to record a nebula on a thirty-minute exposure and was contentedly pottering about, wearing his new glasses, while the photographic plate absorbed light which had begun its journey to Earth before man's ancestors had discovered the use of the club. A stray impulse caused him to glance into the auxiliary sighting scope to check that the main instrument was exactly following its target, and—momentarily forgetful—he did so without removing his low-light spectacles.

Thornton was a modest man in his early sixties, soft-spoken and free of commercial ambition, yet like all other quiet watchers of the skies he had a hankering for the discreet immortality which is granted to the discoverers of new stars and planets. He experienced a moment of heart-lurching giddiness as he saw the first-magnitude object perched on the horizontal cross-hair of his scope, like a diamond where no diamond had any right to be. Thornton stared at the bright speck for a long time, assuring himself it was not a man-made satellite, then became aware of an annoying blue fuzziness in his vision. He tried to rub his eye and his knuckles encountered the frame of the magniluct spectacles. Clucking with impatience, he threw the glasses aside and looked into the sighting scope again.

The bright object was gone.

An insupportable weight of disappointment bore down on Thornton as he checked the luminous settings of the telescope to make sure he had not accidentally jarred the mounting. It was just as he had positioned it except for the minute creeping of the clockwork slow-motion drive. Unable to relinquish hope, he detached the camera from the main telescope, slipped in a low-power eyepiece and looked through it. The nebula he had been photographing was centred in his field of view—further proof that the telescope had not been jolted—and there was no sign of Thornton's Star, as the object might later have been listed in the catalogues.

Thornton's shoulders drooped as he sat in the darkness and deliberated on his own foolishness. He had allowed himself to get worked up, as other astronomers had done before, over an errant reflection in his equipment. The night air whispering through the open sector of the dome suddenly seemed colder, and he recalled that it was past two in the morning. It was an hour at which a man of his age should have been warmly bedded down for the night. He looked around for his magniluct glasses, put them on and—in the blue radiance they seemed to create—began gathering up his notebooks and pens.

It was a whim, a brief refusal to accept the dictates of common sense, which caused him to turn back to the telescope. Still wearing the glasses, he put his eye to the sighting scope. The new star glittered on the cross-hair as before.

Thornton crouched at the sighting scope for a full minute, alternately viewing with the glasses and without them, before fully accepting the phenomenon of a star which could be seen only through a magniluct screen. He took the glasses off and held them in unsteady fingers, feeling the embossed lettering of the trade name—AMPLITE—on the plastic frame, then came the urge to have a fresh, and clearer, look at his discovery. He manoeuvred himself on to the low stool and looked through the eyepiece of the big refractor. There was the unavoidable lack of definition associated with a magniluct transparency, but the object was plainly visible, looking exactly as it had done in the low-powered finder scope. Strangely, it was no brighter.

Thornton's brow creased as he considered the implications of what he was seeing. He had expected the object to appear much more brilliant, due to the light-gathering power of the main telescope's twenty-centimetre lens. The fact that the object looked just the same meant . . . Thornton's mind wrestled with the unfamiliar data . . . that it was emitting no light, that he was seeing it by means of some other type of radiation detected by his Amplite spectacles.

Anxious to make a further check, he struggled to his feet, twisting past the telescope's mounting, and stepped out of the dome on to the pliant turf of his back lawn. The winter night stabbed through his clothing with daggers of black glass. He looked up at the sky and—aided only by the spectacles—selected the region in which he was interested. Coma Berenices was an inconspicuous constellation, but it was one which Thornton had known well since his childhood, and he saw at once the brand-new jewel tangled in the maiden's hair. When he took the glasses off the new star vanished.

At that point Thornton did something which, for him, was very uncharacteristic—he ran towards his house at top speed, careless of the possibility of a twisted ankle, determined to reach his telephone without wasting another second. Many thousands of people throughout the world owned and wore magniluct nightglasses. Any one of them could glance upwards at any time and notice the unfamiliar new object in the heavens—and Thornton had a fierce yearning for it to bear his name.

The past few minutes had been the most exciting in his forty years of practical astronomy, but the night held one more surprise for him. In the utter darkness of the house he put the glasses on again, rather than switch on a light, and made his way to the telephone in the hall. He picked up the handset and punched in the number of an old friend, Matt

Collins, who was professor of astronomy at the University of North Carolina. While waiting for the connection to be made, Thornton glanced upwards in a reflex action which aimed his gaze in roughly the same direction as he had been pointing his telescope.

And there, glittering like a blue diamond, was his special star, as clearly visible as if the upper part of his house, with its beams and rafters and tiles, consisted of nothing more substantial than shadows. As long as he wore the magniluct glasses, the new star could be clearly seen—shining through solid matter with undiminished brilliance.

☆

Doctor Boyce Ambrose was doing his best to salvage a bad day.

He had awakened early in the morning with, as sometimes happened, a gloomy sense of failure. One annoying aspect of these moods was that he had no way of predicting their arrival, or even of knowing what caused them. On most days he felt reasonably pleased with his post as director of the Karlsen planetarium, with its superb new equipment and constant stream of visitors, some of them VIPs, some of them attractive young females anxious to hear everything he knew about the heavens, even to the extent of encouraging his discourses to continue through to breakfast the following morning. On most days he enjoyed the leisurely administrative routine, the opportunities constantly afforded by local newsmen to pontificate on every event which took place between the limits of the stratosphere and the boundaries of the observable universe, the round of social functions and cocktail parties at which it was rare for cameras not to record his presence as he went about his business of being tall, young, handsome, learned and rich.

Occasionally, however, there came the other days, the ones on which he saw himself as that most despicable of creatures —the trendy astronomer. These were the days when he recalled that his doctorate had been awarded by a university known to be susceptible to private financial grants, that his thesis had been prepared with the aid of two needy but scientifically qualified "personal secretaries" engaged by his father, that his job at the planetarium had been up for grabs by anyone whose family was prepared to sink the greatest amount of money into buying the projection equipment. In his extreme youth he had been taken with the idea of proving he could carve out a career with no assistance from the Ambrose fortune, then had come the discovery that he lacked the necessary application. Had he been poor it would have been much easier for him to put in the long hours of solitary study, he eventually reasoned, but he was handicapped by being able to afford every possible distraction. Under the circumstances, the only logical thing to do was to use the money to counteract its effect on his academic career, to buy the things it prevented him from winning.

Ambrose was able to live happily with this piece of rationalisation inplanted beneath his skin—except on the bad days when, for example, an incautious glance at one of the scientific journals would confront him with equations he should have been able to comprehend. On those occasions he often resolved to bring his work at the planetarium up to a new level of efficiency and creativity, and that was why he had made an early three-hour drive to see Matt Collins in person instead of simply contacting him by televiewer.

"I'm not an expert on this thing," Collins told him as they sipped coffee in the professor's comfortable tan-coloured office. "It was a pure coincidence that Thornton and I were old friends and that he rang me first. In fact, I doubt if there is such an animal as an expert on Thornton's Planet."

"Thornton's Planet." Ambrose repeated the words as he felt a pang of jealousy towards the small-town amateur whose name was going into astronomical history merely because he had nothing better to do than spend most of his nights in a tin shed on his back lawn. "We know for sure that it is a planet?"

Collins shook his massive head. "Not really—the word doesn't have much relevance in this case. Now that it has begun to exhibit a disk we've been able to estimate its diameter at about 12,000 kilometres, so it's of planetary size, all right. But, for all we know, in its own frame of reference it might be a dwarf star or a comet or . . . anything."

"What about surface features?"

"Don't know if it has any." Collins sounded perversely happy with his lack of knowledge. He was a giant of a man who seemed impervious to worries which might beset normal-sized individuals.

"My problem is that I have to find some way to represent it at the planetarium," Ambrose said. "What about a magniluct telescope? Can't they make lenses with that stuff?"

"There's no problem with making lens *shapes* out of magniluct material. They would serve pretty well if they were used as nothing more than light amplifiers—but they won't work if you try to obtain a magnified image of Thornton's Planet."

"I don't get it," Ambrose said despairingly, deciding to admit his ignorance. "I'm the director of a planetarium, and I'm supposed to be an instant expert on everything that happens up there, and I don't know what the hell this is all about. Reporters have begun to call me every day and I don't know what to say to them."

"Don't worry about it—there are a lot of so-called experts in the same boat." Collins gave a smile which softened his rough-hewn features. He took two cigars from the pocket of his white shirt and flipped one across the desk to Ambrose. "If you've got time, I'll give you a quick run-down on what little I know."

Grateful for the other man's diplomacy, Ambrose nodded his head as he unwrapped the cigar which he did not really want. "I've got lots of time."

"Okay." Collins ignited both cigars and leaned back, causing his chair to creak loudly. "First of all, I wasn't giving you double-talk about magniluct lenses."

"I didn't think you . . ."

Collins raised a large pink hand, commanding silence. "I've got to get the physics over in one burst because it's all new to me and I only know it up here and not down here." He tapped his forehead and chest in succession, and began to recite.

"Magniluct is a transparent material with a high density of hydrogen atoms in it. There were reports some time ago that it might be useful as a kind of super scintillator to detect neutrinos, but as far as I know nobody took much interest in that aspect until Thornton's Planet came blundering into the Solar System. The planet isn't radiating on any of the known energy spectra—that's why you can't see it in the ordinary way—but it's pumping out neutrinos in four-pi space. When a neutrino enters a lens of your magniluct glasses, it interacts with protons and produces neutrons and beta-plus particles which excite other atoms in the material and in turn produce emissions in the visible region.

"That's why you can't focus the radiation and get a magnified image—the neutrinos go through in a straight line. In fact, it's only because of forward scattering of particles that you're able to see that slightly blurry image of the planet at all. How did I do?" Collins looked like a schoolboy seeking praise.

"Very well," Ambrose said, "especially if particle physics isn't your field."

"It isn't."

Ambrose decided against mentioning that nucleonics had been his own field in case it became apparent that he knew less than might reasonably have been expected. He tapped the first striated section of ash from his cigar and thought hard about what he had just been told.

"This emission of nothing but neutrinos," he said slowly. "I take it that was the basis for deciding that Thornton's Planet is composed of anti-neutrino matter?"

"So I'm told."

"Which means it's a kind of a ghost world. As far as we're concerned, it almost doesn't exist."

"Correct."

"Just my luck," Ambrose said with a wry smile. "How am I going to show it in the planetarium?"

"That, I'm pleased to say, is your problem and not mine."

Collins spoke in sympathetic tones which contrasted with the form of words he had chosen. "Would you like to see where the intruder is at present?"

"Please."

Ambrose sucked gently on his cigar while Collins tapped an instruction into the computer terminal on his desk, calling up an astronomical diagram on the wall screen. As the picture appeared he became aware that the big man was watching him with covert interest, as though hoping for some kind of reaction on Ambrose's part. Ambrose studied the screen which showed two dotted green lines, designated as the orbits of Jupiter and Mars, sliced across by a solid red line representing the path of Thornton's Planet. The diagram was pretty well what he had expected to see, and yet there was a wrongness about it . . . something connected with the mass of data which had just been presented to him . . .

"This is a corrected plan view, normal to the plane of the ecliptic," Collins said, his eyes intent on Ambrose's face. "We've been getting positional fixes on the planet by triangulation and they're fairly accurate because we've been using the Moon colony as the other end of our baseline. The effective length keeps changing, of course, but . . ."

"Hold on," Ambrose snapped, abruptly realising what was wrong with the computer chart. "The red line is curved!"

"So?"

"Well, an anti-neutrino world wouldn't be affected by the sun's gravity. It should sail right through the Solar System in a dead straight line."

"You picked up on that one rather quickly," Collins said. "Congratulations."

Ambrose derived no pleasure from the compliment. "But what does it mean? The diagram suggests that Thornton's Planet is being captured by the sun, but—from what we know about the planet—there's no way that could happen. Are they sure it is an anti-neutrino world?"

Collins hesitated. "If there are any doubts on that score, they'll be resolved in a few months' time."

"You sound pretty sure about that," Ambrose said. "How can you be so certain?"

"It's quite simple," Collins said soberly. "As far as we can determine at this stage, there's every chance that Thornton's Planet is going to pass right through the Earth."

CHAPTER TWO

On the morning of March 25, 1993, Gilbert Snook—the human neutrino—was sitting in a bar, quietly enjoying a cigarette and a suitably chill gin-and-water. He was a lean man of medium height, with black crew-cut hair and neat, hard features. The unusually crisp definition of his muscles, even those around his mouth, suggested physical power, but otherwise his appearance was unremarkable.

His sense of contentment derived from a combination of factors, one of them being that he was having his first day of idleness in two weeks. In the daytime temperatures of the lower Arabian Peninsula the maintenance of light aircraft was an occupation which induced a fine appreciation of luxuries such as merely being cool. Inside the metal shell of a plane the heat was unbearable—metal surfaces had to be covered with rags to stop them inflicting burns, and engine oil thinned out so much that experienced mechanics threw away manufacturers' viscosity recommendations and chose lubricants which would have behaved like treacle in normal circumstances.

The working conditions in Malaq discouraged most foreign technicians from staying long, but they suited Snook's temperament. It was one of several statelets which had been formed after the break-up of the ancient Sultancy of Oman, and the principal attraction to Snook was that it contained only about two people per square kilometre. The mental pressures he disliked in densely populated areas were virtually absent in Malaq. It was even possible for him to avoid newspapers, fax sheets and broadcasts. All that was required of him was his assistance in keeping the ruler's small fleet of military transports and ageing jet fighters in an airworthy condition, in return for which he was accommodated in the country's only hotel and given a generous tax-free salary. Habitually, he sent most of the money to a bank in his native Ontario.

The day had begun well for Snook. He had awakened fresh from a long sleep, enjoyed a western-style breakfast, drifted in the swimming pool for a couple of hours, and now was having a pre-lunch drink. The airfield and native township, five kilometres away, were hidden behind a low headland, making it easy for Snook to convince himself there was nothing in the whole world but the hotel, the broad blue ocean, and the scimitars of white sand curving away on each side of the bay. From time to time he thought about the date he had that evening with Eva, an interpreter with a German engineering consultancy in the town, but for the moment he was concentrating on becoming mildly and happily drunk.

He was puzzled, therefore, to discover a sense of unease growing within himself as the sun passed its zenith. Snook had learned to trust his premonitions—he sometimes suspected he was slightly prescient—but as he looked around the spacious and almost empty lounge he could think of nothing which might have triggered subconscious alarms. From his seat at the window, Snook could see into a small storeroom behind the bar and he was surprised to notice the white-coated barman going into it and putting on what appeared to be a pair of magniluct low-light spectacles. The barman, a suave young Arab, stood perfectly still for a moment, staring upwards, then put the glasses away and returned to the counter where he whispered something to the black-skinned floor waiter. The waiter's eyes flared whitely in his African face as he glanced apprehensively at the ceiling.

Snook took a ruminative sip from his drink. Now that he thought of it, he had noticed a group of European visitors carrying magniluct glasses at the swimming pool and had wondered briefly why they wanted low-light spectacles amid such searing brilliance. At the time it had seemed just another example of the peculiarities which afflicted over-civilised human beings, but other thoughts were beginning to stir.

This was close to the end of May, Snook recalled with effort, and some important astronomical event was almost due. He had no interest in astronomy and, from overhearing conversations among the pilots, had gleaned only a vague notion about the approach of some large but tenuous object, less substantial than the gaseous tail of a comet. When he had learned that the object could not even be seen, except through some tricky property of magniluct glasses, Snook had classed it as little more than an optical illusion and had dismissed it from his mind altogether. It seemed, however, that other people were intensely interested, and this was yet another proof that he was out of step with the rest of humanity.

He took a long swallow from the misted crystal of his drink, but found that his feeling of unease had not been dispelled—there was nothing new in the realisation that he marched to the sound of a different drum. The midday intoxication he had been savouring abruptly vanished, much to his annoyance. He got to his feet and stood at the long window, narrowing his eyes against the influx of light from sand, sea and sky. The European party was still grouped at the screened pool. For a moment he considered going to them and asking if there had been a recent development he should know about, but that would involve him with unnecessary human contacts and he decided against it. He was turning away from the window when he noticed the dust cloud of a vehicle approaching at speed from the north, the direction in which lay the town and airfield. In less than a minute he was able to discern that it was a jeep painted with the desert camouflage of the Sultan's armed forces.

That's it, he thought, oddly satisfied. *That one's for me.*

He returned to his seat, lit a fresh cigarette and tried to guess what had happened. From past experience, it could be anything from one of the jet engines having swallowed a bird, wrecking its metallic digestion in the process, to a faulty warning light on the Sultan's private Boeing. Snook settled down further into the upholstery and made up his mind that he would refuse to respond to any so-called emergency unless it was a matter of life or death. He had just finished his cigarette when Lieutenant Charlton, a pilot in the Skywhip flight, strode into the lounge, red-faced and bristling in his wheat-coloured uniform. Charlton was an Australian of about thirty, who was on a three-year contract to fly fighter planes and who had less feel or regard for machinery than any other man Snook had ever met. He came straight to Snook's table and stood with his bare gold-haired knees pressed against the white plastic. His eyes were pink-stained with rage.

"Why are you sitting here drinking, Snook?" he demanded.

Snook considered the question calmly. "I prefer it to standing drinking."

"Don't be . . ." Charlton took a deep breath, apparently deciding on a change of approach. "Didn't the desk clerk give you my message?"

"He knows better," Snook said. "This is my first day off in two weeks."

Charlton stared helplessly at Snook, then lowered himself into a chair and looked cautiously around the bar before he spoke. "We need you out at the field, Gil."

Snook noted the use of his first name and said, "What's the trouble, Chuck?"

Charlton, who always insisted on ground crew addressing him formally, closed his eyes for a second. "There's a riot brewing up. There's a chance of some of the planes being wrecked and the C.O. has decided to move them up country until things calm down a bit."

"A riot?" Snook was mystified. "Everything was quiet when I left the field yesterday."

"It sprang up overnight—you should know what the Malaqi are like by this time."

"Well, what about the Sultan's militia? What about the *firquat?* Can't they control it?"

"It's the bloody *firquat* who are stirring things up." Charlton wiped his brow. "Gil, are you coming or are you not? If we don't get those aircraft out of there in one hell of a hurry there aren't going to *be* any aircraft."

"If you put it like that . . ." Snook stood up at the same time as Charlton. "It won't take me a minute to change."

Charlton caught his arm and urged him towards the door. "There's no time. This is a come-as-you-are party."

Thirty seconds later Snook found himself in the passenger seat of the jeep and hanging on tightly as it took off in a spurting shower of gravel. Charlton brought the vehicle out on to the coast road in a barely-controlled power drift and drove northwards at top speed, accelerating to the limit in each gear. A hot wind, so different to the air-conditioned coolness of the hotel, roared under the tilted windscreen and made Snook's breathing difficult, while the barren ramparts of the *jebel* shimmered beyond the plain to his left. It came to Snook that he had allowed himself to be bulldozed into giving up a well-earned rest period, and into taking a ride with a dangerously reckless driver, without actually learning the reason for it all.

He tugged Charlton's sleeve. "Is this thing worth getting killed for?"

"Not in the slightest—I always drive like this." Charlton's spirits appeared to have picked up now that he was accomplishing his mission.

"What's the riot all about?"

"Don't you ever listen to the news?" Charlton took his eyes off the road to scan his passenger's face and the jeep wandered close to the encroaching sand and boulders.

"No. I've got other ways of making myself miserable."

"Perhaps you're wise. Anyway, it's Thornton's Planet that's causing all the fuss. Not just here—there's trouble flaring up everywhere."

"Why should there be trouble? I mean, the planet doesn't really exist, does it?"

"Would you like to try explaining that to the average Australian bushman? Or even to the average Italian housewife? The way a lot of people figure it out is that . . . *whoops!*" Charlton broke off to swing the jeep back into the centre of the road, then resumed shouting above the rush of air. "People like that reckon that if you can see it coming, you'll feel it when it gets here."

"I thought you couldn't see it without Amplite glasses."

"Those things are *everywhere* now, sport. Biggest growth industry since they invented sex. In poorer areas the importers snap them in half and sell them off as monocles."

"I still don't get it." Snook contemplated the jouncing horizon for a few seconds. "How can they get worked up over a kind of optical illusion?"

"Have you had a look at it yourself recently?"

"No."

"Here." Charlton felt in his breast pocket, took out a pair of blue-tinted glasses and handed them to Snook. "Have a look up there . . . about due east."

Snook shrugged and put the glasses on. As he had expected, the sunlit sea appeared intolerably brilliant through the special lenses, but the sky was somewhat darker. He tilted his face upwards—and his heart seemed to lurch to a standstill. Thornton's Planet glared down on him, a vast hurtling ball, somehow frozen in its deadly descent, dominating the whole sky with its baleful blue radiance. An ageless and superstitious dread gripped Snook, paralysing his reason, warning him that all the old orders were about to be swept away. He snatched the glasses off and returned to a world of reassuring normalcy.

"Well?" Charlton looked maliciously amused. "What did you think of our optical illusion?"

"I . . ." Snook searched the sky again, overjoyed at its emptiness, striving to cope with the idea of two separate realities. He half-raised the glasses, with the intention of putting them back on, then changed his mind and handed them to Charlton. "It looked real."

"It's just as real as the Earth, but at the same time it's less real than a rainbow." Charlton bounced in his seat like a horseman calling for more speed. "You've got to be a physicist to understand it. *I* don't understand it, but I'm not worried because I trust anybody with letters after his name. These people don't think the same way, though. They think it's going to destroy the world." He gestured towards the wooden huts at the outskirts of the township which was coming into view beyond the diagonal line of a hill. Black-hooded women and small children could be seen among the patch-work buildings.

Snook nodded, filled with a new understanding now that he had looked into an alien sky. "They're bound to blame us, of course. We made the thing visible, therefore we made it exist."

"All I know," Charlton bellowed, "is that we've got to move some aeroplanes and we haven't enough pilots. You could handle one of the old Skyvans, couldn't you?"

"I haven't got a licence."

"Nobody'll give a tinker's about that. This is your chance for a medal, sport."

"Great," Snook said gloomily. He tightened his hold on the jeep's handgrips as Charlton turned off the coast road on to a track which bore west of the town and ran directly to the airfield. Charlton made no concession to the poorer driving conditions and Snook found it difficult to avoid being thrown from the vehicle as it hammered its course among stones and potholes. He was glad when the airfield's perimeter fence came into view, and relieved to see that only a handful of men in Malaqi costume had gathered at the entrance gate, al-though most of them were carrying modern rifles which denoted they were members of the Sultan's militia. As the jeep approached the gate he saw there were other Malaqi in the uniform of regular soldiers positioned inside the fence with their rifles at the ready. His hopes that the situation was less urgent than Charlton had said began to fade. Charlton sounded a long blast on the horn and waved one arm furiously to clear the way ahead.

"You'd better slow down," Snook shouted to him.

Charlton shook his head. "If we slow down too much we won't get through."

He kept going at high speed until they were close to the entrance and white-robed figures leapt to each side with angry cries. Charlton braked hard at the last possible moment and swung the jeep in between two scrapped aircraft tail fins which served as gateposts. It was looking as though his tactics had proved completely successful when an elderly Arab, who had been standing on top of a large oil drum, jumped down in front of the vehicle with upraised arms. There was no time for Charlton to react. A pulpy impact shook the jeep and the old man disappeared beneath its front end. Charlton skidded to a halt beyond the protective line of soldiers and looked at Snook with indignant eyes.

"Did you see that?" he breathed, his face losing its colour. "The stupid old bastard!"

"I think we killed him," Snook said. He twisted in the seat, saw that a knot of men had gathered around the fallen body, and began to descend from the jeep. A bearded sergeant appeared from nowhere and roughly pushed him back into the vehicle.

"Don't go back there," the sergeant warned. "They will kill you."

"We can't just . . ." Snook's words were lost as Charlton gunned the engine and the jeep, snaking its rear end, accelerated towards the line of hangars on the south side of the runway. "What are you doing?"

"The sergeant wasn't joking," Charlton told him grimly, and as if to punctuate his words there came an irregular burst of small arms fire. Sand fountained briefly in several places close to the jeep.

Snook sank down in his seat, trying to make himself into a smaller target, while reluctantly conceding that Charlton—although wrong-headed in many other things—was right in this respect. There were so few cars in Malaq that its people had never come to accept the inevitability of road fatalities. The relatives of an accident victim always treated his death as a case of wilful murder and, even in normal times, set out to gain revenge. Snook knew one aircraft fitter who had accidentally run over a child the previous year and who had been smuggled out of the country by air the same day to preserve his life.

He sat up straight again as the jeep passed into the shelter of a line of revetments and finally came to a halt outside the single-storey building which housed the operations room.

Squadron Leader Gross, an ex-RAF man who was deputy commander of the Sultan's Air Force, came running out to meet them. He paused, wordlessly, while three Skywhip jet fighters took off in formation from the nearby strip. His clean-shaven face was streaked with dust.

"I heard some firing," he said, as soon as the thunder of the jets had receded. "What happened?"

Charlton shifted uneasily and stared at his hands which were clenched on the steering wheel. "They were shooting at us, sir. One of the locals . . . ah . . . got in the way as I was coming in through the gate."

"Dead?"

"He was pretty old."

"Trust you, Charlton," Gross said bitterly. "Christ Almighty! As if things weren't bad enough!"

Charlton cleared his throat. "I managed to find Snook, sir. He's agreed to fly a Skyvan out."

"There are only two Skyvans still here—and they're not going anywhere." Gross pointed into the shade of the nearest hangar where two of the boxy old aircraft were sitting. The starboard propeller of one had chewed through a wingtip of the other, apparently as a consequence of inept taxi-ing at close quarters.

Snook jumped down on to the hot concrete. "I'll have a look at the damage."

"No, I'm moving all civilian personnel up north till this blows over. You'd better go with Charlton in his Skywhip." Gross fixed Charlton with an unfriendly stare. "I wish you a safe journey."

"Thank you." Snook turned and ran behind Charlton who was already halfway to the waiting jet. He climbed into the rear seat and put on the intercom headset while Charlton spun up the engine. The aircraft surged forward almost at once, jolting solidly on its undercarriage, and wheeled on to the runway. Snook was still struggling with his safety straps when the rumbling shocks coming up through the airframe abruptly ceased, letting him know they were airborne. He examined his clothing—dark blue silk shirt, pale blue shorts and lightweight sandals—shocked at its incongruity amid the functional machinery of the cockpit. His watch showed the time to be 01.06, which meant that only nine minutes earlier he had been sitting in the hotel with his watered gin.

Even for Gil Snook, the human neutrino, the uncommitted particle of humanity, the pace of events had been bewildering. He tightened the last buckle, raised his head and saw at once that they were flying south. Not wanting to jump to conclusions, he waited until the aircraft had levelled off at 7,000 metres without changing course before he spoke to the pilot.

"What's the idea, Chuck?" he said coldly.

Charlton's voice was crisp and unabashed in the headphones. "Look at it this way, sport—we're both finished in Malaq. That old scarecrow who jumped out in front of us probably had thirty or forty sons and nephews, and no matter where you go they'll be potting at you with their Martinis and Lee-Enfields. Most of them are lousy shots, but they'll get in close enough some day and it won't do you any good to explain you were just a passenger. Believe me, I know about these things."

"So where are we going?"

"I've finished flying for Gross anyway. We're supposed to be a strike force and all we do is . . ."

"I asked you where we're going."

Charlton's hand appeared above the rim of his ejector seat, the index finger pointing straight ahead in the direction of flight. "There's the whole of Africa to choose from."

Snook shook his head in disbelief. "My passport is back in my hotel room. Where's yours?"

"Back in my quarters." Charlton sounded supremely confident. "But don't worry about a thing—we're within range of at least six brand-new republics where they'll be glad to give us asylum. In exchange for the aircraft, of course."

"Of course." Snook glanced upwards into the eastern sky, frowning. Thornton's Planet was invisible and unreal, but—like any other spectre in the heavens—it had been an omen of ill luck.

CHAPTER THREE

By the Spring of 1996 the passage of Thornton's Planet was fading from the memories of those peoples who had been most alarmed at the time of its close approach to Earth. It had actually passed through the cosmic needle's eye which was the space between the Earth and the Moon, but—as various authorities had predicted—the physical effects had been zero as far as the man in the street was concerned. As the object had dwindled in size to that of any other planet, so had its significance shrunk for the average human being who continued to be faced with the task of remaining alive in an increasingly hungry and factious world. Thornton's Planet could still be seen by anybody who chose to put on magniluct glasses and search for it, but the novelty of sometimes being able to look downwards and observe a blue star shining up through the entire bulk of the Earth remained just a novelty. It provided neither food nor warmth, and was of no other practical value—therefore it was relegated to the same category of astronomical curiosities as auroras and falling stars.

The situation was different in the world's scientific community. The very nature of the celestial intruder hampered its observation and study, but long before Thornton's Planet swept past the Earth it had become obvious that it was being captured by the sun. Angling down through the plane of the ecliptic, it had plunged inside the orbit of Mercury, gaining speed all the while, swung around the sun, then had retreated back through the dim outer limits of the Solar System. Its behaviour was not quite compatible with that of a planet made of normal hadronic matter, but calculations showed that it had adopted a highly elliptical precessing orbit with a period of little more than twenty-four years. The elements of the orbit were such that the planet was expected to revisit the Earth when it had completed four revolutions, that is, in slightly less than a century after its first pass.

This information had a mixed reception among scientific
workers of many disciplines, all of whom—given the available
data as a theoretical exercise—would have predicted that an
anti-neutrino body should pass on through the Solar System
in a straight line, completely unaffected by the sun's gravitic
pull. Most were appalled at seeing the entire citadel of human
science threatened by a casual, heedless visitor from infinity;
others were uplifted by the new challenge to man's intellect.
And a few totally rejected the interpretation of the data, denying that Thornton's Planet could have any objective reality whatsoever.

For his part, Gilbert Snook knew beyond any shadow of
doubt that Thornton's Planet genuinely existed. He had
looked into its livid, blind face, and he had experienced the
devastation of his whole way of life.

There were a number of things which Snook disliked about
his new career in the nine-years-old republic of Barandi,
although—he was compelled to admit—many of the problems
had been of his own making. The first of these had arisen
within one minute of the Skywhip rolling to a standstill on
Barandi's principal military airfield on the northern shore of
Lake Victoria.

Lieutenant Charlton, after some fast talking on the local
communications band, had managed to arrange a sympathetic
reception for himself. And when it was realised he was making Barandi the gift of a well-maintained counter-insurgency
aircraft, plus his own services as a pilot, the reception was
elevated to a state ceremony in miniature, with several high-
ranking officers and their ladies present.

The belated discovery of diamonds in western Kenya had
caused local acceleration of a world-wide process—the breaking up of countries into smaller and smaller political units as
strong centralised government became impossible. Barandi
was one of several new statelets in the region which were
poised on the brink of legality, and it was hungry for defence
equipment which would consolidate its position. Conse-
quently there had been a distinct atmosphere of self-
congratulation, almost of gaiety, among the resplendent

group which assembled to greet the benefactors who were swooping down out of the northern skies.

Unfortunately, Snook had marred the occasion by turning to Charlton as soon as they were both on the ground and felling him with the hardest single punch he had ever thrown. Had it been his intention simply to induce unconsciousness he would have gone for Charlton's solar plexus or chin, but he had been gripped by an overwhelming desire to mess up the pilot's face, and therefore had hit him squarely between the eyes. The result had been two black panda-patches and an enormously swollen nose which had gone a long way towards spoiling Charlton's public image of a clean-cut young airman.

That had been almost three years earlier, but—on days when his spirits were at a low ebb—Snook could still get a boost from remembering how Charlton's social activities had been curtailed by his grotesque appearance during the first week in his adopted country.

His own life had been even more restricted, of course. There had been two days in prison while Charlton was making up his mind not to bear a grudge; a day of interrogation about his political attitudes; and a further month of confinement after he had made it clear that he was not going to service the Skywhip or any other Barandian aircraft. Finally he had been released, warned against trying to leave the country, and—in view of his engineering qualifications—given a job teaching illiterate tribesmen who worked the deep mines west of Kisumu.

Snook believed his post was something of a fiction, created as part of a scheme to give Barandi status in the eyes of UNESCO, but he had devised a workable routine and had even discovered certain aspects of the life which he could enjoy. One of them was that there was a plentiful supply of a superb Arabic coffee, and he made a practice of drinking four large cups of it every morning before thinking about work.

This was the part of the day, just at dawn, during which he most enjoyed being alone, so when the noise of a disturbance at the mine head reached him he doggedly continued with his fourth cup. The trouble, whatever it was, did not seem too serious. Against a background hubbub of voices there was a single high-pitched yammer which sounded like one man indulging in hysterics. Snook guessed that somebody had contracted a fever or had been drinking too much. Either way it was not his concern—picking up bugs and falling down drunk were almost national pastimes in Barandi.

The thought of alcohol reminded Snook of his solitary excesses of the previous night. He left the bungalow's small kitchen, went into the living room and retrieved two empty gin bottles and a glass. The sight of the second bottle brought a momentary pang of dismay—he was fairly certain both had not been full on the day before, but the fact that there was a lingering doubt was proof enough that he was drinking far too much. It was coming near the time for him to move on to another part of the world, regardless of passport or other difficulties.

Snook went out to the back and ceremonially smashing the green bottles into the other glittering fragments in his rubbish bin when he realised he could still hear the lone voice in the distance, and for the first time he sensed the fear in it. Once again he felt the familiar yet ever-strange stirrings of prescience. There was the sound of footsteps at the side of the house and George Murphy, a superintendent at the mine, came hurrying into view. Murphy was a black man, a former Kenyan, but the new Barandian nationalism scorned the use of Swahili names as a relic of the past, on a level with performing tribal dances and carving wooden souvenirs for tourists, and every citizen had an Anglian name for official and general use.

"Good morning, Gil." Murphy's greeting seemed relaxed, but the heaving of his chest beneath the silvercord shirt showed he had been running. His breath smelled of mint chewing gum.

"*Jambo*, George. What's the problem?" Snook replaced the lid of the bin, covering his trove of artificial emeralds.

"It's Harold Harper."

"Is he the one who's making all the fuss?"

"Yes."

"What is it? A touch of the horrors?"

Murphy looked uneasy. "I'm not sure, Gil."

"What do you mean?"

"Harper doesn't drink much—but he says he saw a ghost." Murphy was a mature, intelligent man and it was clear that he was embarrassed by what he was saying, yet was determined to see it through.

"A ghost!" Snook gave a short laugh. "It's amazing what you can see through the bottom of a glass."

"I don't think he was drinking. The shift foreman would have noticed."

Snook's interest quickened. "You mean he was in the mine when it happened?"

"Yes. Coming off night shift on the bottom level."

"What did this . . . ghost look like?"

"Well, it's hard to get much sense out of Harper the way he is at the moment . . ."

"You must have some idea. Are we talking about a lady in a long white dress? Something like that?"

Murphy shoved his hands deep into his trouser pockets, hunched his shoulders and rocked on the balls of his feet. "Harper says a head came up out of the rock floor then sank back into it again."

"That's a new one on me." Snook was unable to resist being callous. "I knew a guy once who used to see long-necked geese walking out from under his bed."

"I told you Harper wasn't drinking."

"You don't have to be swigging right up to the minute the DTs start."

"I wouldn't know about that." Murphy was beginning to lose his patience. "Will you come and talk to him? He's badly shaken up and the doctor's away at Number Four."

"What good would I do? I'm not a medic."

"For some reason Harper looks up to you. For some reason he thinks you're his friend."

Snook could see the superintendent was growing angry, but his own reluctance to become involved was just as strong as ever. Harper was a member of several of his classes and on a few occasions had stayed behind to discuss points of special interest to him. He was a willing student, but many of the

miners were hungry for knowledge and Snook failed to see
that he should therefore be put on stand-by, ready to go running each time one of them bloodied his nose.

"Harper and I get on all right," Snook said, digging in. "I
just don't think I can help him in a case like this."

"I don't think so, either." Murphy's voice, as he turned to
leave, showed his disgust at Snook's attitude. "Perhaps
Harper is just a crazy man. Or maybe there's something
wrong with his Amplites."

Snook suddenly felt cold. "Wait a minute. Was Harper
wearing Amplites when he saw this . . . thing?"

"What difference does it make?"

"I don't know—it seems odd, that's all. How can anything
go wrong with magniluct glasses?"

Murphy hesitated. He obviously realised he had caught
Snook's interest and was taking revenge by being meagre
with his information. "I don't know what can go wrong with
them. Flaws in the material, maybe. Funny reflections."

"George, what are you talking about?"

"This isn't the first incident we've had this week. On Tuesday morning a couple of men coming off the night shift said
they saw some kind of a bird flying around on the bottom
level. If you ask me, they *had* been on the bottle." Murphy
began to move away. "I won't take up any more of your
time."

Snook thought about the unmanning dread he had felt during the one moment, almost three years earlier, when he had
looked on the blotched, glowering face of Thornton's Planet
at its closest to Earth. An instinct prompted him to wonder if
Harold Harper, similarly unready, had made contact with the
unknown.

"If you wait till I get my boots on," he said to Murphy,
"I'll go down to the mine with you."

Barandi National Mine No. 3 was one of the most modern
in the world, and had few of the trappings associated with
traditional-style diggings. The main shaft was perfectly circular in cross-section, having been sunk by a track-mounted

parasonic projector which converted the clay and rock within its beam to monomolecular dust. Apart from the various hoist mechanisms, the dominant feature of the mine head was the snaking cluster of vacuum tubes which drew away the dust created by hand-held projectors on the working levels. It was then piped off to a nearby processing plant where, as a by-product, it formed the basis of high-quality cement.

One thing the mine had in common with all others yielding the same precious material was a very strict security system. His work as a teacher allowed Snook to move freely in the outer circle of administrative buildings and stores, but he had never before been through the single gate in the fence which surrounded the mine head itself. He looked about him with interest as the armed guards examined his identification. A military jeep bearing the star-and-sword emblem of the Barandian government was parked at the miner check-out shed.

Snook pointed the vehicle out to Murphy. "Royal visit?"

"Colonel Freeborn is here. He visits us about once a month to check the security procedures in person." Murphy slapped his own jaw lightly in annoyance. "We could have done without this trouble today of all days."

"Is he a big man with a dent in the side of his skull?"

"That's right." Murphy looked curiously at Snook. "Have you met him?"

"Just once—quite a while ago."

Snook had been interviewed by several army officers during his one day of interrogation after arriving in Barandi, but he remembered Colonel Freeborn most clearly. Freeborn had questioned him in detail about his reasons for refusing to work on Barandian aircraft, and had nodded thoughtfully each time Snook had given a deliberately obtuse answer. In the end Freeborn had said, with perfect candour, "I'm an important man in this country, a friend of the President, and I have no time to waste on white foreigners, least of all you. If you don't start giving plain answers to my questions, you'll leave this office with a skull like mine." He had reinforced his meaning by picking up his cane and fitting the gold ball at its top neatly into the cup-shaped depression on his shaven head. The little demonstration had persuaded Snook that his wisest course would be one of co-operation, and it still rankled with him that he had been cowed so thoroughly within the space of ten seconds. He thrust the memory aside as being unproductive.

"I don't hear Harper now," he said. "Perhaps he's calming down."

"I hope so," Murphy replied. He led the way across rutted hard clay to a mobile building which had a red cross on its side . . . They went up the wooden steps and into a reception room which was bare except for some utility chairs and World Health Organisation posters. Harold Harper, a broad-shouldered but very thin man in his mid-twenties, was slouched in one of the chairs, and two seats away—maintaining his professional detachment—was a black male nurse with watchful eyes. Harper gave a lopsided smile when he saw Snook, but did not speak or move.

"I had to give him a shot, Mister Murphy," the nurse said.

"Without the doctor being here?"

"It was Colonel Freeborn's order."

Murphy sighed. "The Colonel's authority doesn't extend to medical situations."

"Are you kidding?" The nurse's face was a caricature of indignation. "I don't want no dent in my head."

"Perhaps the shot was a good idea," Snook said, going forward and kneeling in front of Harper. "Hey, Harold, what's been going on? What's all this about a ghost?"

Harper's smile faded. "I saw a ghost, Gil."

"You were in luck—I've never seen one of those things in my whole life."

"Luck?" Harper's gaze slid away, seeming to focus on something far beyond the confines of the small room.

"What exactly did you see, Harold?"

Harper spoke in a dreamy voice, occasionally lapsing into Swahili. "I was down on Level Eight . . . far end of the south pipe . . . started to run out of yellow clay, kept hitting rock . . . needed to reset my projector, but I knew it was near the end of the shift . . . turned back and saw something on the floor . . . a little dome, like the top of a coconut . . . shining, but I could see through it . . . tried to touch it—nothing there . . . took off my Amplites for a better look, you know how you do it, automatic like, but there's hardly any light down there . . . without the glasses I couldn't see a thing . . . so I put them on again . . . and . . . and . . ." Harper stopped speaking and began to take heavy, measured breaths. His feet moved slightly, as though a signal to flee was not being fully suppressed.

"What did you see, Harold?"

"There was a head . . . my hand was inside the head."

"What sort of head?"

"Not human . . . not like an animal . . . about this size . . ." Harper crooked his fingers as though holding a football. "Three eyes . . . all together near the top . . . mouth near the bottom . . . my hand was inside the head, Gil. Right inside it."

"Did you feel anything?"

"No. I just got back from it. I was up against the end of the pipe. I couldn't get away . . . so I just sat there."

"Then what happened?"

"The head turned round a bit . . . the mouth moved, but there was no sound . . . then it sank down into the rock. It was gone."

"Was there a hole in the rock?"

"There was no hole in the rock." Harper looked mildly reproachful. "I saw a *ghost*, Gil."

"Could you show me the exact spot?"

"I could." Harper closed his eyes, and his head rolled slightly. "But I sure as hell won't. I'm not going down there again. Not ever . . ." He leaned back in the chair and began to snore.

"You! Florence Nightingale!" Murphy jabbed the nurse's shoulder with a broad forefinger. "How much stuff did you shoot into this man?"

"He'll be all right," the nurse said defensively. "I've sedated men before."

"He'd better be all right, man. I'll be back every hour or so to check—so you'd better bed him down and look after him."

The superintendent, big and competent in his expensive silvercords, was genuinely concerned about Harper, and—uncharacteristically for him—Snook felt the sudden warmth of liking and respect.

"Listen," he said, as soon as they got outside, "I'm sorry I was so slow off the mark up at my place. I didn't realise what Harper was up against."

Murphy smiled, completing the human link. "Okay, Gil. You believed what he told you?"

"It sounds crazy, but I think I do. It was the bit about the glasses that did it. When he took them off he couldn't see the head, or whatever it was."

"That made me think there was something wrong with the glasses."

"It made me think that what Harper saw is very real, though I can't explain it. Do all the miners wear Amplites?"

"They're standard issue. They cut lighting bills by ninety per cent—and you know the energy situation now that they're giving up on the nuclear power plant."

"I know." Snook narrowed his eyes, watching the sun begin its vertical climb from behind the mountains due east. One of the things he disliked about living on the equator was that there was so little variation in the sun's daily path. He imagined it wearing a groove in the firmament, getting into a rut. A line of men had formed at the entrance to the hoist, on their way to go on shift, and Snook became aware that a number of them were grinning and waving at him. One proffered his yellow safety helmet and pointed at the mine entrance, and others near him burst out laughing as Snook gave an exaggerated shake of his head.

"They seem in good form," Snook said. "Most of them aren't so chirpy in class."

"They're scared," Murphy told him. "Rumours spread fast in a mining camp and the two men who thought they saw birds on Tuesday morning have been talking their heads off. This story of Harper's has gone round the camp already, and when he gets into the bar tonight and has a few drinks . . ."

"What are they scared of?"

"Ten years ago most of these men were herders and

farmers. President Ogilvie rounded them up like their own cattle, gave them all Anglo names, banned the Bantu languages in favour of English, dressed them up in shirts and pants—but he hasn't changed them in any way. They never liked going down the mines, and they never will."

"You'd think that after ten years . . ."

"As far as they're concerned, it's another world down there. A world they've no business to enter. All they need is a hint, just one hint, that the rightful inhabitants of that world are objecting to their presence and they'll refuse to go back into it."

"What would happen then?"

Murphy took a pack of cigarettes from his shirt pocket and gave one to Snook. They both lit up and gazed at each other through complex traceries of smoke.

"This single mine," Murphy said, "produced more than forty thousand metric carats last year. What do you think would happen?"

"Colonel Freeborn?"

"That's right—Colonel Freeborn would happen. Right now the government pays the men a living wage . . . and provides facilities like medical aid, even though there's only one qualified doctor serving four mines . . . and free education, even though the teacher is an out-of-work aircraft mechanic . . ." Murphy's eyes twinkled as Snook performed a stiff bow.

"The system doesn't cost much, and the President's advisers get what propaganda value they can out of it," Murphy continued, "but if the miners tried refusing to work, Colonel Freeborn would introduce another system. This has always been good slave country, you know."

Snook studied his loosely-packed aromatic cigarette for a moment. "Aren't you taking a bit of a risk by talking to me like this?"

"I don't think so. I take care to know the man I speak to."

"It's nice of you to say that," Snook replied warily, "but would you be insulted if I went on thinking you must have a reason?"

"Not insulted—disappointed, perhaps." Murphy gave a

high-pitched chuckle which seemed incompatible with his solid torso, and the minty smell of his breath reached Snook. "The men like you because you're honest. And because you're nobody's fool."

"You're still being nice to me, George."

Murphy spread his hands. "What I've been saying is relevant. Look, if you will investigate this ghost thing and come up with some reassuring explanation the men will accept it. And you'll be doing them a big favour."

"Anything that teacher says must be true."

Murphy nodded. "In this case, yes."

"I'm interested." Snook turned to face the steel-framed structures which covered the entrance to the three-kilometre vertical shaft. "But I thought visitors weren't allowed down there."

"You're a privileged case. I talked to Alain Cartier, the mine manager, a while ago and he has already signed the special authorisation."

CHAPTER FOUR

Snook had requested that lighting should be kept to a minimum, and as a result the darkness at the end of the south pipe on Level Eight was almost complete. He felt as though he was standing in a well of black ink which not only robbed him of light but drained all the warmth from his body. There was a flashlight attached to his belt, but the only relief he permitted himself from the pressure of night was occasionally to touch the display stud on his wrist watch. The fleeting appearance of the angular red numerals, telling him that dawn was approaching the world above, also created an illusion of heat. He felt a gentle touch on his arm.

"What'll we do if nothing happens?" Murphy's voice, although he was standing only two paces away, was almost inaudible.

Snook grinned in the blackness. "There's no need to whisper, George."

"Damn you, Snook." There was a pause, then Murphy repeated his question in a voice which was very slightly louder than at first.

"We come back tomorrow, of course."

"Then I'm bringing a hot water bottle and a flask of soup."

"Sorry," Snook said. "No heat sources—one of the cameras has infrared film in and I don't want to chance spoiling the results. Photography isn't one of my fields."

"But you think a magniluct filter will work on a camera?"

"I don't see why it shouldn't. Do you?"

"I see bugger all," Murphy whispered gloomily. "Even with my Amplites on."

"Keep them on—just before dawn seems to be the most likely time for an appearance, if there's going to be one."

Snook was wearing his own low-light glasses and, like Murphy, could see almost nothing. The magniluct lenses were designed to amplify meagre scatterings of light to a level at which the wearer's surroundings became visible, but where there was less than a threshold level their performance was uncertain. He leaned against the end wall of the pipe, constantly moving his eyes, determined not to miss the slightest manifestation of anything unusual, and occasionally took the Amplites off for a second to compare the two forms of vision. Perhaps ten minutes had passed when Snook began to think he could sense a slight difference—it seemed to him that the blackness was less intense while he was looking through the glasses. No shapes were visible, not even a localised variation in the near-luminance, and yet he became almost certain his field of view was infinitesimally brighter, as if a faintly luminous gas was seeping into the tunnel.

He said, "George, do you notice anything?"

"No." The other man's reply was immediate.

Snook cursed his lack of proper equipment. He had no way of proving that the apparent increase in brightness was not due to the sensitivity of his eyes improving with the long stay in darkness. Suddenly a speck of light, faint as a minor star, appeared at his left and wandered lazily across his vision. Snook pushed the button which, by means of a device he had built during the day, operated the shutters of four cameras.

The multiple clicks and the sound of the winding-on mechanisms were shockingly loud in the taut blackness. He checked the time by his watch and memorised it.

"Did you see that?" he said. "A thing like a small firefly?"

There was a moment of silence, then Murphy said, "Gil—look at the floor!"

A spot of dim light appeared on the floor and gradually became a disk. When the circle was as large as a man's hand, Snook became aware that he was in fact looking at a transparent luminous dome, tufted on top like a coconut. He fought to control his breathing, and by an effort of will operated the cameras again. Within seconds the dome had risen and enlarged itself into a roughly spherical object resembling a head upon which travesties of human lineaments were barely visible. The body below it glowed *within* the rock.

There were two eyes near the top, and between them—only slightly lower down—was a third hole which might have been a nose, unadorned by nostrils. No ears were visible, and very close to the bottom was a slitted mouth, tremendously wide and mobile. Even as Snook watched, the mouth twitched and writhed, assuming compound curvatures and quirks which—on a man's face—would have indicated an interplay of feelings ranging from boredom to anger to amusement to impatience, plus others for which there were no human counterparts.

The sound of Murphy's harsh breathing reminded Snook that he still had a job to do. He took another set of photographs and, without conscious thought, kept on operating the cameras every few seconds as the apparition steadily rose higher, coming more completely into view.

The alien head was followed by narrow, sloping shoulders and strangely jointed arms which emerged from a complicated arrangement of robes, frills and straps, made more intricate by the fact that they were semi-transparent and thus could be glimpsed at the back of the figure as well as at the front. Shadowy organs slid and pulsed internally. The creature continued to rise through the floor at the same steady pace, in utter silence, until it was fully in view. It stood about the height of a small man, on two disproportionately thin legs which were hazily seen amid the hanging folds of its robes. The feet were triangular and flat, displaying radial arrays of bones among which wove the thongs of what appeared to be sandals.

When the creature had emerged fully into the tunnel it turned slightly and, in a curiously human gesture, raised one hand to its eyes as if shading them from a bright light. It gave no indication of being aware of the two men. Snook's powers of reasoning were all but obliterated by a pounding dread, yet he discovered he still had capacity for further surprise. Conditioned by the physical laws of his own existence, he had expected the glowing figure to cease its upward movement when it was on a level with himself, but it continued rising at the same unchanging rate until its head passed into the tunnel roof. The head was followed into the solid rock by the rest of the blue-sketched translucent body.

Spreading outwards horizontally from the plane of its feet, like an insubstantial floor, was a surface of radiance which also travelled upwards, creating the illusion that the tunnel was filling with glowing liquid. When its level passed above Snook's eyes he found himself blinded with cloudy luminescence and in sudden panic he snatched off the Amplite glasses.

The tunnel plunged into its former state of utter darkness, and for a moment Snook found himself trembling with relief at the sheer luxury of not being able to see anything. He stood perfectly still for a time, breathing heavily, then turned on his flashlight.

"How's it going, George?" he said tentatively.

"Not too well," Murphy replied. "I feel sick."

Snook gripped Murphy's arm and urged him away from the end wall of the pipe. "So do I, but we'd better save it for later."

"Why?"

"I don't know how high our visitor intends to go, but I think you should get the men out of the level above this one. If they see what we just saw the mine will close down for ever."

"I . . . What do you think it was?" Murphy sounded as

though he wanted Snook to produce an immediate scientific label for the apparition and render it harmless.

"It was a ghost, George. By most of the classical definitions it was a ghost."

"It wasn't human."

"Ghosts aren't."

"I mean it wasn't the ghost of a human being."

"There's no time to worry about that now." Snook put his Amplite glasses on again and found his vision still filled with a cloudy radiance which partially obscured details of what he could see in the tunnel, even with the flashlight on. He took them off and checked the time on his watch. "Let's see . . . this pipe is about two metres high and the thing we saw went up through it in about six minutes."

"Was that only six minutes?"

"That's all it was. Is there a pipe directly above this one?"

"Only the whole Seven-C system, that's all."

"How far?"

"Varies according to the shape of the clay deposits—could be only five or six metres in some places." Murphy's voice was mechanical, remote. "Did you notice its feet? They were like a bird's feet. A duck's feet."

Snook shone his light directly into Murphy's eyes, trying to irritate him into coming to grips with the problem. "George, if the thing keeps rising at the same speed it'll be on the next level in maybe less than ten minutes. You should get the men out of there before that happens."

Murphy covered the light with his hand, fingers redly translucent. "I haven't the authority to take the men out."

"All right—just stand back and watch them take themselves out. I've got to look after these cameras."

"There's going to be a panic." Murphy was suddenly alert. "I'd better get on the phone to the mine manager. Or even the Colonel." He switched on his own handlight and began hurriedly picking his way over the vacuum pipes which curved along the floor.

"George," Snook called after him, "the first thing to do is get the men to take off their Amplites and make their way

out by ordinary light. That way they won't see anything unusual."

"I'll try."

Murphy passed out of sight around a curve in the tunnel
and Snook busied himself with the task of dismantling his improvised camera equipment. In the absence of proper tripods
he had set the four cameras up on a small folding table. He
was working as quickly as possible in the hope of transport-
ing everything to a higher level in time to intercept the ghost
again, but it was cold in the tunnel and his fingers refused to
function properly. Minutes passed before he had loaded the
cameras and the connecting servos into a cardboard carton,
gathered up the table and set off in the direction of the main
shaft. He had just reached the continuous elevator when the
first panic-stricken shouts began to echo down from above.

The electric lighting was stronger on the Level Eight gallery which surrounded the shaft, but Snook was severely
hampered by his load and almost missed his footing as he
stepped into one of the ascending cages. He steadied himself
against a steel mesh wall and made ready to get out at Level
Seven-C. The shouting grew louder during the few seconds it
took to reach the next gallery, and as Snook was leaving the
cage he found his way blocked by three men who were pushing their way in. They jammed the exit momentarily, each
clawing the other back. By the time Snook had forced his
way out the cage had risen more than a metre above the rock
floor and he made an awkward bone-jarring landing, drop-
ping the table in the process.

Other miners, most of them wearing Amplites, had surged
out of the south tunnel and were already fighting their way
into the succeeding cage. Snook heard the lightweight table
splintering beneath their boots.

Protecting his carton of photographic equipment, he
breasted the tide of frightened men until he had reached a
clear space at the entrance to a pipe which was not being
worked. Breathing heavily, he felt in his pocket for his
magniluct glasses and put them on. His picture of his surroundings instantly flared into brightness and he saw that he

and the other men on the gallery were apparently waist-deep in a pool of radiance. Snook thought of it as a kind of floor on which the spectral visitor stood, and the sight of it confirmed what he already knew from the behaviour of the miners—that the creature had penetrated to Level Seven.

"Take off your Amplites," he shouted to the men who were milling around the elevator, but his voice was lost in the aural flux of shouts and grunts. Snook decided against trying to make his way into the south tunnel in case his cameras got smashed. He stood with his back to the wall, waiting for the steadily-moving elevator to carry the miners up to the surface, then became aware of another facet of the ghostly phenomenon. The plane of bluish radiance, the phantom floor, was sinking back towards the level of the rock floor. As he watched, the two levels merged and—coincidentally—the exodus of men from the south pipe abruptly ceased.

Snook darted into the tunnel and found that it veered quite sharply to the west. He swung around the first bend, ran along a lengthy straight section with its tangle of vacuum pipes and discarded projectors, and reached a second bend. When he got round it he stumbled to a halt.

Here, at least ten of the luminous figures were visible.

All were sinking into the floor at a noticeable rate, but in addition these beings had lateral movement. They were walking, with a curious turkey-like gait, some of them in pairs, emerging from one wall of the tunnel and fading into the other. The complex transparencies of their robes swirled around the thin legs as they moved; the eyes—too close to the tops of the tufted heads—rolled slowly; and the impossibly wide slits of mouths, alien in their degree of mobility, pursed and twisted and reshaped in silent parodies of speech.

Snook, paralysed with awe, had never seen anything so essentially alien, and yet he was reminded of textbook illustrations of ancient Roman senators strolling and conversing at their leisure about matters of empire. He watched for the several minutes that it took for the figures to sink down into the tunnel floor, until only the glowing heads were visible moving purposefully through the skeins of vacuum tubes, until finally there was nothing to be seen but the normal evidences of human existence.

When the last luminous mote disappeared it was as if a clamp had been released from about his chest. He took a deep breath and turned away, anxious to get back to the surface world and its familiar perspectives. On his way to the elevator it occurred to him that he had not tried to photograph the alien scene, and that the chance to do so would probably recur were he to go back down to Level Eight. He shook his head emphatically and kept walking at a steady pace to the elevator, clutching his box of cameras. The circular gallery was deserted when he got there, and he had no difficulty in stepping into an empty cage. At Level Four two young miners—one of whom was in Snook's English class—jumped into the cage with him. They were glancing at each other and smiling nervously.

"What been happen, Mister Snook?" said the boy who was in Snook's class. "Somebody say we all go to a special meet up top. Others all go *pesi*."

"Nothing much happened," Snook told him in a matter-of-fact voice. "Some people have been seeing things, that's all."

Stepping out of the cage into a bright morning world of sunshine, colour and warmth gave Snook a powerful sense of reassurance. Life, it seemed, was continuing exactly as usual regardless of what terrors lurked beneath the ground. It took Snook a few seconds to appreciate that a tense and highly abnormal situation was developing within the mine head enclosure. Perhaps two hundred men were gathered outside the check-out building, from the steps of which Alain Cartier was addressing them in an angry mixture of English and Swahili, laced here and there with expletives in his native French. Some of the miners were giving their attention to Cartier, others were engaged in group arguments with various supervisors who moved among them. The management were putting across the message that it was the duty of the miners to return to work without further delay; while the latter—as Snook and Murphy had predicted—were refusing to go underground.

"Gil!" Murphy's voice came from close by. "Where have you been?"

"Having another look at our transparent visitors." Snook scanned the superintendent's face. "Why?"

"The Colonel wants to see you. Right now. Let's go, Gil." Murphy was almost dancing in his impatience and Snook began to feel an obscure anger at the men, and the power they wielded, which could affect other and better human beings in that way.

"Don't let Freeborn buffalo you, George," he said with deliberate stolidity.

"You don't understand," Murphy replied in a low, urgent voice. "The Colonel has already sent to Kisumu for troops—I heard him on the radio."

"And you think they'd fire on their own people?"

Murphy's gaze was direct. "The Leopard Regiment is stationed at Kisumu. They'd massacre their own mothers if the Colonel gave the word."

"I see. And what am I supposed to do?"

"You have to make Colonel Freeborn believe you can smooth things over and get the men back to work."

Snook gave an incredulous laugh. "George, you saw that thing down there as well as I did. It was *real*. There's no way anybody can convince those men it didn't exist."

"I don't want any of them to get killed, Gil. There's got to be some way." Murphy pressed the back of a hand to his mouth in a childlike gesture. Snook felt a pang of sympathy which surprised him with its intensity. *It's happening*, he thought. *This is the way you get involved*.

Aloud he said, "I've got an idea I can put up to the Colonel. He might listen, I suppose."

"Let's go and see him." Murphy's eyes signalled gratitude. "He's waiting in his office."

"Okay." Snook walked several paces with the superintendent, then stopped and clutched his lower abdomen. "Bladder," he whispered. "Where's the lavatory?"

"That can wait."

"Want to bet? Listen, George, I don't make a good advocate when I'm standing in a pool of urine."

Murphy pointed at a low building which had red flowers growing in window boxes. "That's the supers' rest room. Go in there. First door on the left. Here—I'll hold the cameras for you."

"It's all right." Snook walked quickly to the door of the building, went through to the toilets and was glad to find them empty—it appeared that the disorderly meeting was keeping the supervisors busy. He locked himself in a cubicle, set his carton on the toilet seat, picked up the camera which had been fitted with a magniluct filter and took out its spool of self-developing film. A quick glance at it showed him that the improvised technique had been successful—there were surprisingly clear images of the first apparition he had seen—and he dropped the spool into his pocket. Working as swiftly as he could, Snook put a fresh film in the camera, pressed the palm of his hand over the lens to block out all light, and pushed the shutter button twelve times, producing the same number of exposures as were in the other cameras. He put the camera back in the box, flushed the toilet and went outside to where Murphy was waiting.

"That took long enough," Murphy grumbled, his composure fully recovered.

"It doesn't do to rush these things." Snook handed the box of cameras and equipment to the superintendent, dissociating himself from it. "Now where's Führer Freeborn?"

Murphy led the way to another prefabricated building which was partly screened by oleander bushes. They went into a reception room, where Murphy spoke quietly to an army sergeant who was seated at a desk, and then were ushered into a larger room which was given a vaguely military atmosphere by the presence of numerous maps on the walls. Colonel Freeborn was exactly as Snook had remembered him—tall, lean, hard as the polished teak of which he seemed to be carved, somehow managing to appear meticulously neat and rough-shod at the same time. The cup-shaped depression glistened at the side of his shaven skull. He looked up from the paperwork he had been studying and focused on Snook with intent brown eyes.

"All right," he snapped, "what have you found?"

"And a very good morning to you, too," Snook said. "Are you well?"

Freeborn gave a tired sigh. "Oh, yes—I remember you. The aircraft engineer with principles."

"I don't care about principles—I just don't like being shanghaied."

"If you remember, it was your friend Charlton who brought you to Barandi. I simply offered you a job."

"And refused me permission to leave."

"Worse things have happened to men who entered this country illegally."

"No doubt." Snook eyed the cane with the spherical gold knob which lay on the desk.

Freeborn got to his feet, went to the window and stood looking out towards where the miners' meeting was still in progress. "I have been informed that you have done valuable educational work among the labour force at this mine," he said in a surprisingly mild voice. "It is very important, at this stage, that the education of the miners should continue. In particular, it should be impressed on them that ghosts do not exist. Primitive beliefs can be harmful . . . if you know what I mean."

"I know what you mean." Snook was about to announce that he preferred the Colonel not to try being subtle, when he intercepted a pleading glance from Murphy. "But there's nothing I can do about it."

"What do you mean?"

"I've just been down to the bottom levels. The ghosts do exist—I've seen them."

Freeborn spun on his heel and pointed an accusing finger. "Don't try it, Snook. Don't try to be clever."

"I'm not being clever. You can see them for yourself."

"Right! I'd be very much interested in that." Freeborn picked up his cane. "Take me to see the ghosts."

Snook cleared his throat. "The snag is that they only appear shortly before dawn. I don't know why it is, but they rise up into the bottom levels of the mine around dawn. Then they sink down out of sight again. They seem to be rising higher each day, though."

"So you can't show me these ghosts?" Freeborn's lips twitched into a smile.

"Not now, but they'll probably appear tomorrow morning again—that seems to be the pattern. And you'd need to be wearing Amplite glasses."

Aware of how incredible his story sounded, Snook went on to describe everything he had seen and done in the mine, with a full description of the ghosts and of his experimental camera equipment. When he had finished speaking he called upon Murphy to corroborate his statement. Freeborn gave Snook a speculative stare.

"I don't believe a word you've told me," he said, "but I love all the circumstantial detail. You say these day-trippers from Hades are only visible through low-light glasses?"

"Yes—and that's your solution to the whole problem. Issue instructions that every man has to turn in his Amplites and the ghosts won't be seen again."

"But how would the men see to work?"

Snook shrugged. "You'd have to install full-scale lighting the way they did before magniluct was invented. It would be expensive—but a lot cheaper than closing down the mine."

Freeborn raised his cane, in an absent-minded gesture, and its gold head slid naturally into the depression on his skull. "I've got news for you, Snook. There isn't the remotest possibility of the mine being closed down, but I'm still fascinated by this story you've dreamed up. Now, about those cameras— I presume you didn't think of using self-developing film?"

"As a matter of fact, I did."

"Open them up and let me see what you got."

"Suits me." Snook began opening the cameras and removing the spools. "I'm not too happy about the polarised or the infrared, but the one with the magniluct filter should show something if we're in luck." Snook unrolled the spool in question, held it up to the light, and clucked with disappointment. "It doesn't look like there's anything here."

Freeborn tapped Murphy on the shoulder with his cane. "You're a good man, Murphy," he said evenly, "and that's why I'm not going to have you punished for wasting my time today. Now get this lunatic and his cameras out of my office, and never bring him near me again. Have you got that?"

Murphy looked apprehensive, but stood his ground. "I saw something down there, too."

Freeborn flicked his cane. Its weighty head travelled only a short distance, but when it collided with the back of Murphy's hand there was a sound like that of a twig being snapped. Murphy drew breath sharply and gnawed his lower lip. He did not look down at his hand.

"You're dismissed," Freeborn said. "And, from now on, anybody who contributes to the mass hysteria that's been going on here will be regarded as a traitor to Barandi. You know what that means."

Murphy nodded, turned quickly and walked to the door. Snook got to it first, turned the handle for him and they went outside together. The miners' meeting was still in progress and had grown even noisier than before. Murphy raised his right hand and Snook saw that it had already begun to swell.

He said, "You'd better get that seen to—I think you've got a broken bone."

"I *know* I've got a broken bone, but it can wait." Murphy caught Snook's shoulder with his good hand and stopped him walking. "What was all that meant to be about? I thought you had an idea you were going to try out on the Colonel."

"I tried it. Full lighting in the mine . . . no magniluct glasses . . . no ghosts."

"Is that all?" Murphy's face showed his disappointment. "I thought you were going to prove to him that the ghosts were real. You and your bloody box of tricks!"

Snook paused thoughtfully. The more people who knew about his plan the greater the risks would be, and yet he had forged a rare link with Murphy and had no wish to endanger it. He decided to take the chance.

"Look, George." Snook pressed his fingers against the side pocket of his jacket, outlining the film spool within. "When I went into the toilets a while ago I took this film out of one of the cameras and put a new one in its place. This one shows our ghost."

"*What?*" Murphy tightened his grip on Snook's shoulder.

"That's what we needed! Why didn't you show it to the Colonel?"

"Calm down." Snook twisted free of the other man's grasp. "You'll ball the whole thing up if you make too much fuss. Trust me, will you?"

"To do what?" Murphy's brown face was rigid with anger.

"To change the situation. That's your only hope. Freeborn's on top right now because this is his private little universe where he can order a massacre if he wants, and get away with it. If he had seen the evidence that ghosts really exist he would have buried it, and probably us too.

"You saw the interest he took in the cameras. He didn't believe what we told him, but he wanted to look at the film—just in case. It suits people like Freeborn to keep things the way they are, with nobody in the outside world giving a damn about Barandi or anything that happens in it."

"What can you do about that?" Murphy said.

"If I can reach the Press Association man in Kisumu with this film, I promise you that by this time tomorrow the whole world will be looking over Freeborn's shoulder. He'll have to call off his Leopards—and there'll be a chance to find out what our ghosts really are."

CHAPTER FIVE

The day began to go wrong while Boyce Ambrose was having breakfast.

His fiancée, Jody Ferrier, had stayed at his family home near Charleston all week-end, which had been fine with Ambrose except that—in deference to his mother's famous Puritanism—they had had separate bedrooms. The arrangement meant that he had spent more than two days in Jody's company without being able to indulge in any of the love games at which she was so naturally and deliciously good. Ambrose was not oversexed and had not been particularly

disturbed by the two days and three nights of abstinence, but
the experience had focused his attention on an alarming fact.

Jody Ferrier—the girl he had promised to marry—talked a
great deal. Not only did she talk a great deal, but none of the
subjects which engaged her attention was of the slightest interest to him. Furthermore, each time he had tried to divert
the conversation towards more fruitful grounds, she—with
masterly ease—had brought it back at once to fashion trends,
local real estate values, and the genealogies of important
Charleston families. These were the points at which, had they
been alone in one of their apartments, he would have silenced
her with a bout of old-fashioned physical grappling—and,
during the week-end, Ambrose had come to suspect that
what he had been regarding as a richly sexual relationship
had, in fact, been a prolonged struggle to keep Jody quiet.

By Sunday night his forebodings about his planned mar-
riage had reached the pitch at which he had become morose
and withdrawn. He had gone to bed quite early, and in the
morning had found himself actually looking forward to the
day's work at the planetarium. There had, however, been an
unexpected development. Jody was clever, as well as rich and
beautiful, and it appeared that during the night she had correctly deduced his frame of mind. At breakfast she had announced, for the first time since they had met, that she had
always possessed a burning curiosity about all things astronomical and was proposing to gratify it by spending the day
at the planetarium. The idea, once it had germinated, seemed
to blossom in her mind.

"Wouldn't it be wonderful," she had said to Ambrose's
mother, "if there was some way I could help Boyce with his
vocation? On a purely voluntary basis, of course—perhaps for
two or three afternoons a week. Some tiny little job. I
wouldn't care how unimportant it was as long as I was helping to make people aware of the wonders of the universe."

Ambrose's mother had been impressed with the scheme and
thought it was splendid that her son and her future daughter-
in-law shared the same intellectual interests. She was certain
Jody could find something useful to do at the planetarium,
perhaps on the public relations side. For his part, Ambrose

had been disappointed in Jody. He regarded himself as a leading expert on every aspect of pretence—after all, he had made
a career of it—and he had previously felt a grudging respect
for his fiancée's honesty in openly not giving a damn about
his work. *All right,* he had thought, *I'll go along with this
thing . . . provided she never says "light years in the future."*
He had remained quiet during the early part of the drive to
the planetarium, preferring to listen to the radio, and this had
given Jody the chance to demonstrate her cosmic awareness.

"If only people could be made to realise how insignificant
the Earth is," she was saying, "if they would just understand
that it's only a speck of dust in the universe, there'd be less
war and less petty strife. Isn't that so?"

"I don't know," Ambrose replied, determined to be un-
helpful. "It might work the other way round."

"What do you mean, darling?"

"If they start thinking the Earth is insignificant, they could
decide that nothing they do will make any difference to anything and start raping and pillaging even harder."

"Oh, *Boyce!*" Jody laughed incredulously. "You didn't
mean that!"

"I do. Sometimes I worry in case the shows at the planetarium are encouraging the human race to snuff itself out."

"That's nonsense." Jody fell silent for a moment, gauging
Ambrose's mood, and a shift took place in his hearing, bringing the words of a radio newscast to the forefront of his attention.

"*. . . claims that the ghosts are real beings, which can only
be seen with the aid of magniluct low-light glasses. The diamond mine is in Barandi, one of the small African republics
which have not yet been admitted to the United Nations.
Real or not, the ghosts have caused . . .*"

"I've heard you say *dozens* of times that the only real
justification for astronomy is . . ."

"Let me hear this," Ambrose put in.

"*. . . science correspondent says that Thornton's Planet,
which passed close to the Earth in the spring of 1993, is the
only other known example of . . .*"

"That's another thing—your mother says the lectures you gave about Thornton's Planet were the best . . ."

"For God's sake, Jody, I'm trying to hear something."

"Well, all right! There's no need to shout."

". . . *new theories about the atomic structure of the sun. South America. The dispute between Bolivia and Paraguay came one step closer to all-out war last night when . . .*" Ambrose switched the radio off and concentrated on the mechanical tasks of driving. There had been a fall of snow during the night and the road, which had been cleared down to the tarmac, was like a swath of India ink in a scraperboard landscape.

Jody put a hand on his thigh. "Go ahead and listen to the radio—I'll be quiet."

"No you go ahead and talk—I won't listen to the radio." It occurred to Ambrose that he was being unfair. "I'm sorry, Jo."

"Are you always grouchy in the morning?"

"Not every morning. But the trouble with being a trendy astronomer is that I hate being reminded that other people are doing real work."

"I don't understand you. Your work is important."

Jody's hand moved higher on Ambrose's thigh, sending a tingle of sensation racing into his groin. He shook his head, but was grateful for the little intimacy, with its message that there were other values in life besides those of the laboratory. Forcing himself to relax, he tried to enjoy the remainder of the journey to the pleasant modern building in which he worked. The air was sharp and jewel-bright after the snowfall, and by the time they had got from his car to the office at the side of the dome Ambrose was feeling better. Jody was pink-cheeked and fresh, like a girl in a health foods advertisement, and he felt absurdly proud as he introduced her to his secretary and office manager, May Tate.

He left the two women together and went into his private suite to see what communications had filtered through the various systems to reach his desk. At the top of the heap was a fax sheet on which May had put a ring of dayglow ink around one of the main stories. Ambrose read the terse, tongue-in-cheek story of how a Canadian teacher, with the inelegant name of Gil Snook, had gone down a diamond mine in Barandi and taken a photograph of a grotesque "ghost"—and, as he stood there in the warm luxury of his office, he began to feel ill.

Ambrose's sudden lack of well-being stemmed from a number of factors.

There was the guilt he felt about the betrayal of his own academic potential. In the past this guilt had manifested itself as jealously towards the amateur astronomer who, as the reward for years of quiet diligence, had been privileged to attach his name to a star. And here, represented by a few lines of type, was another example of the same kind of thing. How had it come about, Ambrose demanded of himself, that an obscure teacher with a ridiculous name had been at the right place at the right time? And how had this man known to do all the right things, the things which would make him world-famous? There was no mention of Snook having any kind of scientific qualifications—so why had he, of all people in the world, been chosen to make an important discovery?

There was no doubt in Ambrose's mind that what had happened in the backwoods African republic was important, although it was as yet too early for him to say what the significance of the event actually was. The news story contained two items which clamoured in his thoughts—and one of these was that the ghostly sightings happened just before dawn. Ambrose was good at geography, and therefore he knew that Barandi straddled the Earth's equator.

As an astronomer, regardless of his trendiness, he also knew that the Earth was like a vast bead sliding along the unseen wire which was its orbit. The wire did not enter and leave the surface of the globe at fixed positions, as with an ordinary bead—these two points wove a lazy curve up and down the Earth's torrid zone as the planet completed a daily revolution on its axis. And at this time of the year, late winter in the northern hemisphere, when it was dawn in Barandi—and the ghosts were walking—the "forward" orbital intersection point would be passing invisibly through the tiny republic. Every instinct Ambrose possessed told him there was no element of coincidence involved.

The second news item was that the apparitions were visible only with the aid of magniluct glasses, and in Ambrose's opinion this linked them in some way with the passage of Thornton's Planet almost three years earlier.

He sat down at his desk, filled with a sense of imminence, feeling cold and sick and yet curiously elated. Something was happening inside his head, right behind his eyes, a strange and rare event he had only read about in connection with a few other men. He folded his arms on the deep-glazed wood of the desk, lowered his forehead to rest on them, and remained absolutely still. For the first time in his life, Doctor Boyce Ambrose was encountering the phenomenon of inspiration. And when he raised his head he knew exactly why it was that apparitions had begun to appear in the lower levels of Barandi National Mine No. 3.

Jody Ferrier entered his office a minute later and found Ambrose white-faced and chill behind his desk. "Boyce, darling!" Her voice was taut with concern. "Are you all right?"

He looked at her with bemused eyes. "I'm all right, Jo," he said slowly. "The only thing is . . . I think I have to go to Africa."

The journey to Barandi was a difficult one for Ambrose, even with his money and extensive family connections.

He had originally planned to make an SST flight from Atlanta to Nairobi, and perhaps charter a light aircraft to cover the remaining three hundred kilometres to his destination. This scheme had been scrapped, on the advice of the travel agency, because relations between Kenya and the newly-formed Confederation of East African Socialist Republics were particularly bad at the time. Ambrose had accepted the situation philosophically, remembering that Kenya and other countries had lost valuable territory to the Confederation. He then had aimed for Addis Ababa, only to be told that Ethiopia was on the point of mounting a military operation against the Confederation—to re-establish her southern border—and that all commercial flights between the two were on the point of being suspended.

In the end he had flown in an uncomfortably crowded SST to Dar-es-Salaam in Tanzania, and had been forced to wait seven hours for a place on a shabby turboprop. The latter had taken him to the new "city" of Matsa, in the republic of the same name, which was Barandi's neighbour to the west. Now he was waiting at the airport for a commuter flight to Kisumu, and was beginning to question the impulse which had driven him to leave the States in the first place.

With the advent of the dangerous Nineties, the great age of tourism had ended. Ambrose was a wealthy man and yet had rarely been abroad, and then only to recognised stable countries such as England and Iceland. As he stood in the searing brilliance of the concourse, with its dioramas of mountain ranges and shimmering ferrocrete runways, he could feel a growing xenophobia. Many of the waiting travellers appeared to be journalists or photographers, presumably being attracted to Barandi by the same magnet, but the faint sense of kinship they inspired was more than offset by the frequent sight of black soldiers wearing short-sleeved drills and carrying machine guns. Even the gleaming newness of the building disturbed Ambrose by reminding him that he was in a part of the world where institutions were not revered, where things which were not present yesterday could equally well have vanished by tomorrow.

He had lit a cigarette and was wandering in a lonely little circle, keeping within easy view of his luggage, when he noticed a tall blonde girl looking cool and composed in a white blouse and lime green tailored skirt. She seemed so out-of-place, so much like a fashion plate for expensive British clothes, that Ambrose glanced around half-expecting to see cameras and lighting equipment being set up in the vicinity. The girl was alone, however, and unperturbed by the stares of the heterogeneous males standing nearby. Ambrose, both captivated and filled with the desire to appoint himself protector of the fair lady, was unable to resist staring too. He was filling his eyes with the sight of her when she took out a cigarette, pouted her lips on to it and continued peering into her purse with traces of a frown. Ambrose stepped forward and offered her a light.

"I've seen this happen so many times on old TV movies," he said, "that I feel selfconscious about doing it in real life."

She lit the cigarette, appraising him all the while with calm grey eyes, then smiled. "It's all right—you do it very well. And I did need a smoke." Her accent was English. Well-educated English, Ambrose thought.

Encouraged, he said, "I know the feeling. Hanging around airports depresses me."

"I do it so much that it has ceased to register."

"Oh?" Unused to dealing with British girls, Ambrose tried in vain to assign a background to this one. Actress? Air hostess? Model? Jet setter? He stopped musing when she gave a delighted laugh, showing perfect teeth which had a very slight inward slope. His puzzlement increased.

"I'm sorry," she said, "but you looked so baffled. Perhaps you would like everybody to wear labels showing their occupations."

"I'm sorry. It was just . . ." Ambrose turned away, but she stopped him by touching his arm.

"Actually, I do have a label. A badge, really, but I never wear it because it's a silly thing and the pin destroys my clothes." Her voice had become warmer. "I work for UNESCO."

Ambrose made one of his best smiles. "The badge makes you sound like an investigator."

"You could say I'm a kind of investigator. Why are you going to Barandi?"

"I'm an investigator, too." Ambrose debated with his conscience about claiming to be a physicist or an astronomer, and in the end he added one vague qualifier. "Scientific."

"How interesting! Are you ghost hunting?" The complete absence of mockery in her voice made Ambrose think of the incredulous scorn he had endured from both Jody and his mother when he had announced his plans to visit Barandi.

He nodded. "But right now the only thing I'm hunting is a cold drink. How about you?"

"I'd love one." The girl gave Ambrose a direct smile which

modified all his opinions about Africa, foreign travel and the design of airports. The potential rewards for the globe-trotter, he decided, greatly outweighed the dangers and discomforts. Leaving his luggage to fend for itself, he escorted the girl to the mezzanine bar, feeling boyishly pleased at the resentful glances from men who had witnessed the entire meeting.

Over chilled Camparis with soda he learned that her name was Prudence Devonald. She had been born in London, read economics at Oxford, travelled extensively with her father who was in the Foreign Office, and joined UNESCO three years earlier. Currently she was on secondment to the Economic Commission for Africa, visiting the African states of recent origin who had applied for UN membership and checking that the money they received in the form of educational grants was being spent in an approved manner. Ambrose was intrigued to hear that her trip to Barandi was not a matter of routine, but had been occasioned by the sensational news stories concerning National Mine No. 3. Barandi was promoting itself as one of the most progressive members of the CEASR, with high educational standards for all its citizens. Prudence's office had been surprised, therefore, to hear that a man called Gilbert Snook—who had no listed teaching qualifications, and had been involved in the theft of a military aircraft from another country—apparently was head of the mine school. The affair was a delicate one because there had been pressure from some quarters to suspend educational grants to Barandi. Her brief was to investigate the situation, with special reference to Gilbert Snook, and make a confidential report.

"That's quite a big responsibility for somebody your age," Ambrose commented. "Can it be that, in secret, you're a hardhearted woman?"

"There's no secret about it." Prudence's finely-moulded features assumed an impersonal quality, like those of a beautiful but highly functional robot. "Perhaps we should get it clear that it was I who picked you up a few minutes ago. It didn't happen the other way round."

Ambrose blinked. "Who said anybody got picked up?"

"What would you call it? What's the latest Americanism?"

"All right—why should you want to pick me up?"

"I need a male escort as far as Barandi—to save me the trouble of fending off various undesirables—and I picked you." She took a sip of her drink, grey eyes unyielding above the glassy rim.

"Thanks." Ambrose considered her remarks and found a crumb of comfort. "It's good to know I'm not an undesirable."

"Oh, you're very desirable—much more so than any ordinary scientist."

Ambrose felt an impostor's guilt. "Assuming there is such an animal as an ordinary scientist," he said, "what makes you think I'm not one?"

"In the first place, your wristwatch cost you at least three thousand dollars. Shall I go on?"

"Don't bother." Ambrose was taken aback and unable to prevent himself being pompous. "I'm interested in the value of things, not the price."

"Wilde."

Ambrose floundered for a moment—convinced she had used the word "wild" like a mid-century hipster—then understanding came. "Did Oscar Wilde say that?"

Prudence nodded. "Something like it. In 'Lady Windermere's Fan'."

"That's a pity—I've been going around for years passing it off as my own." He gave her a rueful smile. "Christ knows how many people I've convinced that I'm semi-literate."

"Don't worry about it—I'm sure you've got lots of other qualities." Prudence leaned forward and, unnecessarily, touched the back of his hand. "I like your sense of humour."

Ambrose looked closely at her, made wary by his glimpse of the tough-minded, hard-edged person who inhabited such an essentially female body. Prudence's face had not altered, but he found he could now see it in two different ways, revealing two different characters, as with an op art picture in which shifts of perception changed heights into depths. He was intrigued, impressed and attracted all at once, and for this reason the idea of simply being picked up, used and discarded rankled more than ever.

"What would happen if I refused to chaperone you to Barandi?" he said.

"Why should you refuse?"

"Because you don't need me."

"But I explained that I do need you—to fend off undesirables. That's what chaperones are for."

"I know, but . . ."

"Would you abandon any other girl in the same situation?"

"No, but . . ."

"Then why me?"

"Because I . . ." Ambrose shook his head, lost for words.

"I'll tell you why, Doctor Ambrose." Prudence's voice was low, but firm. "It's because I don't play the old game. You know the one I mean. Every time a helpless female accepts courtesy from a gallant male there's the implication—even though it's rarely taken seriously—that, if everything develops favourably, she'll repay him by making herself available. Now, I like you, and it's possible that if we were in Barandi long enough, and you were keen, that we might go to bed together—but it wouldn't be because you held a door open for me or carried my case on to a plane. Do I make myself clear?"

"Gin clear." Ambrose swallowed a large portion of his drink. "That's a British expression, isn't it?"

"All right—equality isn't fair." Prudence took out another cigarette and accepted a light for it. "Tell me what you're going to do about these ghosts. Are you going to exorcise them?"

"No exorcism is possible in this case," Ambrose said soberly.

"Really? You've got a theory?"

"Yes—I'm here to check it out."

Prudence shivered with an excitement Ambrose found gratifying. "Does it explain why they can only be seen with those special glasses? And why they keep rising up and sinking back into the ground again?"

"Hey! You've really been paying attention to the news."

"Of course! Come on—don't keep me in suspense."

Ambrose cooled his fingertips on the dewy sides of his

glass. "This is a little awkward. You know how an artist doesn't like anybody to see a painting until it's finished? Well, scientists are like that with their pet theories. They don't like making them public until they've tied up every loose end."

"I can understand that," Prudence was unexpectedly docile. "I'll look forward to hearing about it on the radio."

"Ah, hell," Ambrose said. "What difference does it make? I know I'm right. It's a bit involved, but I'll try explaining it to you if you want."

"Please." Prudence moved forward on her chair until her knees were touching Ambrose's.

"You remember Thornton's Planet?" he said, trying to ignore the distraction. "The so-called ghost world that came near the Earth about three years ago?"

"I remember the riots—I was in Ecuador at the time."

"Everybody remembers the riots, but the thing that sticks in the average physicist's craw is that Thornton's Planet was captured by our sun. It's composed of anti-neutrino matter and therefore should have gone through the Solar System in a straight line and never been seen again. The fact that it went into orbit upset a lot of people and they're still trying to dream up whole new sets of interactions to account for it. But the simplest explanation is that inside our sun there's another one composed of the same kind of matter as Thornton's Planet. An anti-neutrino sun inside our hadronic sun."

Prudence frowned. "Underneath the big words, it sounds as though you're saying two things can occupy the same space at the same time. Is that possible?"

"In nuclear physics it is. If a field has a flock of sheep in it does that stop you driving in a herd of cows?"

"Please let's try it without the Will Rogers routine."

"Sorry—it's hard to know how far to go with analogies. What I'm saying is that if there's an anti-neutrino sun centred on our sun there could just as easily be an anti-neutrino planet centred on the Earth. Who is Will Rogers?"

"Before your time. Are you serious about this world within a world?"

"Absolutely. It's slightly smaller than the Earth and that's why, even if magniluct had been around a long time, we would not know about the inner world. Its surface would normally be many kilometres below our ground level."

Prudence dropped her unsmoked cigarette into a pedestal ashtray. "And this inner world is inhabited by ghosts."

"Well, ghosts is a terribly unscientific word, but you've got the idea. To the inhabitants of that world *we* would be ghosts. The big difference is that, because the Earth is bigger, we inhabit their stratosphere—so it's unlikely they would ever have detected us."

"So what happened? Was it something to do with . . . ?"

Ambrose nodded. "Thornton's Planet is composed of the same kind of matter as our inner world, and therefore would have had a strong effect on it. Strong enough to disturb it in its orbit. That's why the inner world has begun to emerge through the Earth's surface—the two worlds are steadily separating from each other." He looked beyond Prudence's rapt, dreaming face and noticed the heat-wavering image of an aircraft on final approach. "I think this is our plane."

"There's no need to hurry—besides, you haven't told me everything."

Prudence was gazing at him with what seemed to be open admiration. Ambrose found himself reluctant to break the spell of the moment, and yet his memory told him there was another Prudence Devonald, self-interested and pragmatic, who might be playing him along for reasons of her own.

"Are you interested in astronomy?" he said.

"Very much."

He grinned. "Do you ever say 'light years in the future'?"

Prudence gave a good-natured sigh. "Is that your own personal *pons asinorum?*"

"I guess so. I'm sorry if I . . ."

"Don't apologise, Doctor. Is it enough to say that a light year is a measurement of distance, or do I have to work it out in metres?"

"What else did you want to know?"

"Everything," Prudence said. "If there's an inner world

coming out through the Earth, as you say, why do the ghosts keep rising up to where they can be seen and then sinking back down out of sight again?"

"I was hoping you wouldn't ask me that."

"Why? Does it hurt your theory?"

"No—but it's hard to explain without diagrams. If you draw a circle, then draw another circle inside it and slightly off centre so that they touch at the left side, it will give you an idea of the current relative positions of the two worlds."

"That seems simple enough."

"It's simple because your diagram is static. The fact is that the Earth turns on its axis once every day—and apparently the inner world does the same—so both your circles should be rotating. If you put a mark at the point where they touch, and rotate both circles, you'll find the mark on the inner circle sinking below the same point on the outer circle. By the time you've given both circles a half turn the inner point will have sunk to its maximum distance below the outer point, then if you go on turning they'll gradually approach each other again. This is why the ghosts have only been sighted around dawn—there's a twenty-four hour wait for your points to coincide again."

"I see." Prudence spoke with the wondering voice of a small child.

"As well as rotating your circles, it's also necessary to keep moving the inner circle to the left. This means that, instead of coinciding once a day, your inner point will begin travelling further and further *outside* the outer point."

"It's beautiful," Prudence breathed. "It all *fits*."

"I know." Again, Ambrose was gratified.

"Are you first with this theory?"

Ambrose laughed. "Before I left home I wrote a couple of letters staking a claim to it, but it will soon be in the public domain. You see, the ghosts are going to spread. Before long they'll be visible on the surface—there'll be no need to go down a diamond mine—then the circle of emergence will grow quite rapidly. At first the sightings will be confined to the equatorial regions, places like Borneo and Peru, then they'll spread north and south through the tropics into the temperate zones."

Prudence looked thoughtful. "That's going to cause some excitement."

"You," Ambrose said, finishing his drink, "are a master of the art of understatement."

CHAPTER SIX

Snook's telephone began to ring and, at the same instant, somebody knocked loudly on the front door of his bungalow.

He went to the living-room window, parted two slats of the blind and peered out. Three black soldiers were standing on the verandah—a lieutenant, a corporal and a private—all wearing the black-and-tan spotted berets of the Leopard Regiment. The corporal and the private had the inevitable submachine guns slung on their shoulders, and they also wore expressions that Snook had seen many times before in other parts of the world. They were examining his house with the appraising, faintly proprietary looks of men who had been authorised to use any degree of force necessary to accomplish their missions. As he watched, the lieutenant pounded the door again and took one step backwards, waiting for it to be opened.

"Hold on a minute," Snook shouted as he went to the telephone, picked it up and gave his name.

"This is Doctor Boyce Ambrose," the caller said. "I've just arrived in Barandi from the States. Has my secretary been in touch with you to explain why I'm here?"

"No. International communications don't operate too well in these parts."

"Oh, well—I expect you can guess what brought me to Barandi, Mister Snook. May I come out to the mine to see you? I'm very much . . ." Ambrose's words were lost in an even louder hammering on the front door. It sounded as though a gun butt was being used, and Snook guessed that the next step would be to burst the door open.

"Are you in Kisumu?" he snapped into the phone.

"Yes."

"At the Commodore?"

"Yes."

"Hang on there and I'll try to contact you—right now I've got some visitors at the door."

Snook heard the beginnings of a protest as he set the phone down, but his principal concern was with the impatient group on his doorstep. He had been expecting some kind of reaction to his publicity campaign from Colonel Freeborn and it remained to be seen how violent the storm was going to be. He hurried to the door and flung it open, blinking in the mid-morning sun.

"You are Gilbert Snook?" The lieutenant was a haughty young man with an angry stare.

"I am."

"It took you a long time to come to the door."

"Well—you were knocking at it for a long time," Snook said with the tricky obtuseness he had been practising for years and which he knew to infuriate officials, especially those whose native tongue was not English.

"That's not the . . ." The lieutenant paused, recognising the danger of involving himself in verbal exchanges. "Come with us."

"Where to?"

"I am not required to give that information."

Snook smiled like a teacher disappointed by a child's lack of comprehension. "Son, I have just required it of you."

The lieutenant glanced at his two men, and his face showed he was reaching a difficult decision. "My orders are to bring you to Kisumu to see President Ogilvie," he said finally. "We must leave at once."

"You should have said so at the beginning," Snook chided. He took a lightweight jacket from a hook, stepped out and closed the door behind him. They went to a canvas-topped jeep, Snook was given a rear seat beside the corporal and the vehicle surged away immediately. Almost at once, Snook saw two Land-Rovers emblazoned with the sign "Pan-African News Services." As they passed the mine-head enclosure he was interested to see that the four armoured cars which had been sitting at the fence the night before were now absent. A number of men were moving through the mine buildings, but the vacuum tubes which snaked away to the south were translucent—instead of opaque with speeding dust—which showed that no excavation was taking place below ground.

Snook knew the mine had never before ceased production for as much as a single day, and he guessed that economic pressures were building up somewhere. The conflict was between the new Africans and the old; between modern ambitions and ancient fears. President Paul Ogilvie and Colonel Freeborn were men of the same breed, adventurers whose nerve and lack of scruples had enabled them to hack a prime cut from the carcase of Africa. Ogilvie, in particular, promoted the notion that Barandi had a wide-based economy—with its exports of pyrethrum flowers and extract, coffee, soda ash and some electronics products—but the diamond mines were what had brought the country into being and were what kept it in existence. Snook could imagine the President's growing rage at the closure of National Mine No. 3.

The interesting thing, however, was that Ogilvie and Freeborn still had no true idea of what they were up against, of the strength of the miners' determination not to go underground again. It was one thing to dismiss the ghosts as a product of mass hysteria, without having seen them; but it was something else to stand in a dark tunnel, kilometres below the surface, and watch the procession of silent, glowing figures with their slow-turning heads and mouths which warped in response to unknown emotions. With the bright morning air flowing around him, and the ambience of a motor vehicle with its sounds and smells and chipped paintwork—the essence of human normalcy, even Snook found it difficult to believe in the ghosts.

He sat without speaking for the whole of the jolting ride into Kisumu and beyond it to the new complex of governmental offices which sprawled over eighty hectares of parkland. The cubist architecture was softened and modified by islands of jacarandas, palms and Cape chestnuts. Positioned near the centre of the complex was the presidential residence. It was surrounded by a small lake which was sufficiently ornamental to disguise the fact that it served the same function as a moat. The jeep passed across a bridge, stopped at the main entrance to the residence, and a minute later Snook was ushered into a room of high windows, oiled woods and Murano glass. President Ogilvie was standing at a desk near one of the windows. He was a man of about fifty, with a thin-lipped, narrow-nosed cast of features which, to Snook's eyes, made him look like a Caucasian in dark stage make-up. His clothing was exactly as in all the pictures Snook had seen of him—blue business suit, white stiff-collared shirt, narrow tie of blue silk. Snook, normally not susceptible to such things, abruptly became aware of the sloppiness of his own clothes.

"Sit down, Mister Snook," Ogilvie said in a dry unaccented voice. "I believe you have already met Colonel Freeborn."

Snook turned and saw Freeborn standing in a shaded corner with his arms folded. "Yes, I've met the Colonel," Snook said, lowering himself on to a chair.

Freeborn uncrossed his arms, long-muscled beneath the half-sleeves of his drill shirt, and the gold head of his cane shone like a miniature sun. "When you speak to the President use the correct form of address."

Ogilvie raised a slim hand. "Forget it, Tommy, we're here to talk business. Now, Mister Snook—Gilbert, isn't it?—you realise we have a problem here. A very expensive problem."

Snook nodded. "I can see that."

"There's a school of thought which holds you responsible."

"I'm not." Snook glanced briefly at Freeborn. "In fact, when I was talking to the school of thought in his office a couple of days ago, I gave him good advice on how to avoid the problem. He wasn't interested."

"What was your advice?"

"The ghosts can be seen only through magniluct glasses. Take the miners' glasses away, install full lighting—no ghosts. It's too late now, of course."

"You still insist that these ghosts really exist?"

"Mister President, I've seen them, and I've photographed them." Snook, who had been leaning forward in his earnestness, sat back and wished he had avoided any reference to the pictures.

"That brings me to another point," Ogilvie said, taking a thin cigar from a box and sitting on one corner of his desk to reach for a lighter. "Colonel Freeborn tells me you took the film from the camera in his presence, and at that time it was blank. How do you explain that?"

"I can't," Snook said simply. "The only thing I can suggest is that the radiation by which we see the ghosts takes a long time to resgister on a negative."

"That's crap," Ogilvie stated unemotionally, examining Snook through smoke-narrowed eyes. Snook received a distinct impression that the preliminaries had ended and that the serious business of the interview was about to begin.

"I don't know much about these things," he said, "but now that scientific researchers have begun to arrive in Kisumu from the States maybe we'll get a better understanding of what's going on."

"Have you spoken to any of these people?"

"Yes—I'm meeting a Doctor Ambrose later today." Snook resisted the temptation to add that it would cause comment if he failed to keep the appointment. He knew that he and Ogilvie were communicating on two levels, one of which required no words.

"Doctor Ambrose." Ogilvie moved behind his desk, sat down and made a note on a writing pad. "As you know, it is my policy to encourage tourists to visit Barandi—but it would be very wrong to entice them to come here with exaggerated ideas of what the country has to offer. Tell me, Gilbert, did you fake those photographs?"

Snook looked shocked. "I wouldn't know how, Mister President. But even if I did know how—why should I?"

"That's another thing I can't understand." Ogilvie smiled his regret. "If I could attribute a motive . . ."

"How did the photographs get into the hands of the Press?" Freeborn put in from his place in the corner.

"Well, *that* was my fault," Snook replied. "I came into

town that night for a drink and ran into Gene Helig, the Press Association man. We got to talking about the ghosts. Then I remembered I had shoved the film spools into my pocket and I took them out. You can imagine the surprise I got when Gene noticed the images on one film."

Ogilvie gave a humourless laugh. "I can imagine."

Snook decided to get back on to firmer ground. "The central issue, Mister President, is that these so-called ghosts do exist and the miners won't go anywhere near them."

"That's what they think," Freeborn said.

"I don't believe in supernatural phenomena," Snook continued. "I think there's bound to be a plain explanation for the things that have been seen, and I think the only efficient way to clear up the whole mess is to find out what the explanation is. The whole world's watching Barandi at this time and . . ."

"Don't belabour the point." Ogilvie had begun to sound bored. "You've stuck your nose into a lot of things without any authority—are you prepared to act as official liaison man if I give permission for a full scientific investigation to be carried out at the mine?"

"I'd be glad to." Snook fought to conceal his surprise.

"All right. Go and see your Doctor Ambrose, and tie in with Cartier, the mine manager. And keep Colonel Freeborn fully informed. That's all." Ogilvie turned his swivel chair and sent a cloud of cigar smoke rolling in the direction of the nearest window.

"Thank you, Mister President." Snook got to his feet and, without looking in the direction of Colonel Freeborn, hurried from the room. The interview with the President had gone better than he could have hoped for, and yet he had an uneasy feeling that he had been out-manoeuvred.

Freeborn waited a few seconds, ensuring that Snook had gone, before he moved forward into the light. "Things are bad, Paul," he said. "Things are bad when a grease monkey like that can swagger in and out of here, laying down the law."

"You think he should be shot?"

"Why waste a bullet? A plastic bag over the head is more satisfactory—it gives them lots of time to repent."

"Yes, but unfortunately our grease monkey—by accident or design—has done all the right things to keep himself alive." President Ogilvie stood up and paced the length of the room, marking his path with blue smoke clouds, and looking like a corporation executive discussing a sales plan. "What do you know of his history?"

"Only that I should have ended it three years ago when I had the chance." Freeborn, in a reflex action, raised his cane and slid its gold head into the dent in his skull.

"There's more to him than you think, Tommy. For instance, the suggestion he gave you about collecting all the miners' low-light glasses had a lot of merit."

"It would have involved a complete new lighting system for the mine. Have you any idea how much that would cost these days? It isn't as if your nuclear power station had begun to work when it was supposed to."

"New lighting would have been a trifle compared to the cost of a major shut-down—in any case, there's more than money involved." Ogilvie wheeled and pointed at the bigger man with his cigar. "Money means very little to me, Tommy. I've got more of it than I'll ever be able to spend. The only thing I really want now is for this country, Barandi, the country that I made, to be given its rightful membership of the United Nations. I want to walk into that building in New York and see my flag up there among all the others. That's why the diamond mines have to keep going. Because without them Barandi wouldn't last a year."

Freeborn's eyes shuttled briefly as he sought the right words to use. He had been exposed to the President's megalomania in the past and had no sympathy with it. The idea of his country's leader dreaming of hoisting a scrap of cloth in a foreign city beyond the ocean—while there were hostile forces on the borders only a matter of kilometres distant— filled him with impatience and dismay, but he was accustomed to concealing his thoughts and biding his time. He had even learned to endure seeing the President take white and

Asian whores to his bed, but a day was approaching when he would be in a position to give Barandi the firm military leadership it cried out for. In the meantime, he had to maintain and consolidate his own power.

"I share your dreams," he said slowly, flooding his voice with sincerity, "but that's all the more reason for us to take decisive steps right now, before the situation deteriorates any further."

Ogilvie sighed. "I haven't gone soft, Tommy. I have no objection to you turning your Leopards loose on the rabble at Number Three—but it can't be done when there are outside observers present. The logical first step is to get them out of the country."

"But you've just given permission for them to go right into the mine."

"What else could I do? Snook was right when he said the whole world is watching us." Ogilvie suddenly relaxed and smiled. He took his cigar box from the desk and offered it to Freeborn. "But the world soon grows tired of watching one part of Africa after another—you should know that as well as I do."

Freeborn accepted a cigar. "And in the meantime?"

"In the meantime I want you—unofficially, of course—to make life difficult for our little scientific community from abroad. Don't do anything obtrusive or newsworthy, just make life difficult for them."

"I see." Freeborn felt a resurgence of confidence in the President. "How about the Press Association man, Helig? Is he to be put out of business?"

"Not now—it's too late to correct that particular mistake. Just watch him in future."

"I'll look after things."

"Do that. And there's something else—we'll have to refuse entry to any further foreign visitors. Find some valid reason to cancel all entry permits."

Freeborn frowned in thought. "Smallpox outbreak?"

"No, that could interfere with trade. It would be better if there was a military emergency. Say, an attack by one of our long-established neighbours. We'll discuss the details over lunch."

Freeborn lit his cigar, inhaled deeply, then smiled with something approaching genuine pleasure. "The Gleiwitz technique? I have a few awkward prisoners in reserve."

President Ogilvie, the image of a corporation executive in his conservative blue suit, nodded his assent. "Gleiwitz."

Freeborn's smile developed into a chuckle. He had never been a student of European history, but the name of Gleiwitz, a speck on the map close to Germany's border with Poland, was familiar to him because it had been the scene of a Nazi operation which both Ogilvie and he had emulated more than once in their own careers. There, in the August of 1939, the S.S. Gestapo had staged a fake Polish attack on the German radio station and—as visible evidence of the crime by their neighbours—had strewn the area with the bodies of men whom they had dressed in Polish army uniforms and then shot. The incident had been used in propaganda as justification for the invasion of Poland.

Colonel Freeborn regarded it as an exemplary piece of military tactics.

Snook's mind was still seething with suspicion about President Ogilvie's reactions when he got out of the taxi at the Hotel Commodore. It was almost noon, and the sun was hanging directly overhead like an unshaded lamp. He plunged into the prism of shadow beneath the hotel canopy, went through the split-level foyer—ignoring a signal from the desk clerk—and straight into the bar. Ralph, the senior barman, saw him coming and without speaking took a quarter-litre glass, half filled it with Tanqueray's gin and topped it up with ice water.

"Thanks, Ralph." Snook sat on a stool, cushioned his elbows on the puffy leather facing of the bar and took a long therapeutic drink from his glass. He felt its coolness travel all the way to his stomach.

"Rough morning, Mister Snook?" Ralph put on the look of rueful sympathy he always used with hangover sufferers.

"Grim."

"You'll feel better after that."

"I know." Snook took another drink. He had enacted the same little tableau, with exactly the same dialogue, many times before and he drew comfort from the fact that Ralph had sufficient empathy never to vary the routine. It was about the only kind of communication Snook enjoyed.

Ralph leaned across the bar and lowered his voice. "Two people over there waiting to see you."

Snook turned in the indicated direction and saw a man and a woman regarding him with dubious expectancy, and the phrase "the beautiful people" sprang into his mind. They were a well-matched couple—both young, immaculate and with finely chiselled, fair-skinned good looks—but it was the woman who held Snook's attention. She was slim, with intelligent grey eyes, full-lipped, cool and sensuous at the same time; and to Snook came a sudden fear that his entire way of life had been a mistake, that this was the sort of prize he might have won had he opted for life in the glittering cities of the occident. He lifted his glass and went towards their table, disturbed at the pang of jealousy he felt towards the man who rose to meet him.

"Mister Snook? I'm Boyce Ambrose," the man said as they shook hands. "We spoke on the telephone."

Snook nodded. "Call me Gil."

"I'd like you to meet Prudence Devonald. Miss Devonald is with UNESCO. Actually, I think she wants to talk business with you, too."

"This must be my lucky day." Snook spoke the words automatically as he sat down, his mind busy with the realisation that the couple were not married, as he had somehow assumed. He saw that the girl was giving him a look of frank appraisal and, for the second time that day, became conscious of the fact that his clothing was barely passable and even then only because the material was indestructible.

"It isn't your lucky day," Prudence said. "In fact, it could be quite the reverse. One of the things I have to do in Barandi is check up on your teaching qualifications."

"What qualifications?"

"That's what my office would like to know." She spoke with a direct unfriendliness which saddened Snook and also goaded him into his standard pattern of reaction.

"You work for an inquisitive office?" He met her gaze squarely. "Do you report to the desk or the filing cabinet?"

"In English," she said, with insulting sweetness, "the word 'office' can also mean the staff who work there."

Snook shrugged. "It can also mean a lavatory."

"I was just about to get us a couple more Homosexual Harolds," Ambrose said quickly to Snook. "You know . . . Camp Harrys. Would you like another drink?"

"Thanks. Ralph knows my tipple." While Ambrose went to the bar Snook leaned back comfortably, looked at Prudence and decided she was one of the most beautiful women he had ever met. If there was anything short of perfection in her face it was that her upper teeth had a very slight inwards slope, but for some reason this served to enhance the aristocratic impression she created in his mind. *I want you*, he thought. *You're a bitch, but I want you.*

"Perhaps we should start over again," he said. "We seem to have got off on the wrong something or other."

Prudence almost smiled. "It's probably my fault—I should have guessed you'd be embarrassed to answer my questions with a third party present."

"I'm not embarrassed." Snook allowed himself to sound mildly surprised at the notion. "And, just for the record, I won't be answering any of your questions."

Her grey eyes triangulated on him angrily, but at that moment Ambrose arrived back at the table with the Camparis and gin. He set them down and examined the accompanying sales slip with a puzzled expression.

"There seems to be a mistake here," he said. "This round cost three times as much as the last one."

"That's my fault." Snook raised his drink in salute. "I order my gin by the beer glass to save trotting back and forwards to the bar." He glanced at Prudence. "I get embarrassed."

Her lips tightened. "I'd be interested to hear how you can drink like that and hold down a job as a teacher."

"I'd be even more interested," Ambrose put in heartily, "to hear your first-hand account of . . ."

Snook silenced him with an upraised hand. "Hold on a moment, Boyd."

"Boyce."

"Sorry—Boyce. I'd be most interested of the lot to hear why this lady keeps quizzing me about my private business."

"I'm with UNESCO." Prudence took a silver badge from her purse. "Which means that your salary comes . . ."

"My salary," Snook interrupted, "consists largely of one crate of gin and one sack of coffee every two weeks. Any hard cash I get I earn by repairing automobile engines around the mine. In between times I teach English to miners on the nights when they've no money left for pleasures of the flesh. These clothes I'm wearing are the same ones they gave me when I came here three years ago. I often eat my dinner straight out of the can, and I brush my teeth with salt. I get drunk a lot, but otherwise I'm a model prisoner. Now, is there anything else you want to know about me?"

Prudence looked concerned, but gave no ground. "You claim you're a prisoner here?"

"What else?"

"How about political refugee? I understand there's the question of a fighter plane which disappeared from Malaq."

Snook shook his head emphatically. "The pilot of the plane is a political refugee here. I was a passenger who thought it was going in the opposite direction, and I'm a prisoner here because I refused to service it for the Barandian Army." Snook was alarmed to discover that he had discarded all his defenses for a woman he had met only a few minutes earlier.

"I'll include this in my report." Prudence held her silver badge closer to her mouth, revealing that it was also a recorder, and her lips developed an amused quirk. "Do you spell your name just the way it sounds?"

"It is a funny name, isn't it?" Snook said, slipping back into character. "How clever of you to decide to be born into a family called Devonald."

The colour rose in Prudence's cheeks. "I didn't mean . . ."

Snook turned away from her. "Boyce, what's going on here? Are you a UNESCO man, too? I came here because I thought you were interested in what we saw at the mine."

"I'm a private researcher and I'm intensely interested in what you saw." Ambrose gave Prudence a reproachful glance. "It was pure coincidence that I met Miss Devonald—perhaps if we arranged separate appointments . . ."

"There's no need—I'm going to shut up for a while," Prudence said, and suddenly Snook saw in her the schoolgirl she had been not many years earlier. He began to feel like a veteran legionary who had chosen to sharpen his sword on a raw recruit.

"Gil, have you any idea of what you actually did see at the mine?" Ambrose tapped Snook's knee to regain his attention. "Do you know what you discovered?"

"I saw some things which looked like ghosts." Snook had just made the more immediate discovery that, in moody relaxation, Prudence Devonald's profile inspired in him an obscure anguish which had to do with the transience of beauty, of life itself. It was his first conscious experience of the kind, and it was not entirely welcome.

"What you saw," Ambrose said, "were the inhabitants of another universe."

It took a few seconds for the words to come to a sharp focus in Snook's mind, then he began to ask questions. Twenty minutes later he leaned back in his chair, took a deep breath, and realised he had forgotten about his drink. He sipped from the glass again, trying to accustom himself to the idea that he was sitting at the crossroads of two worlds. Once more, within the space of a single hour, he was being forced to think in new categories, to make room in his life for new concepts.

"The way you put it," he said to Ambrose, "I have to believe you—but what happens next?"

Ambrose's voice developed a firmness which had not been there earlier. "I should have thought the next step was quite obvious. We have to make contact with these beings—find a way of talking to them."

CHAPTER SEVEN

The news that Ambrose wanted to begin observations that very night did not bother Snook—his own imagination had been fired by what he had heard—but he was irritated by the practical consequences.

Ambrose's theory confirmed that the ghostly appearances would not begin until near dawn, although they would gradually start earlier and finish later each day. The road from Kisumu to the mine was long and difficult, especially for someone who was unfamiliar with it, and Snook had felt obliged to invite Ambrose to stay the night at his bungalow. This was going to involve Snook being in continuous proximity to the other man for the best part of a day and a night, and his nature rebelled against the imposition. The fact that Prudence had invited herself along, clad in a Paris designer's impression of a safari suit, had not made things any better.

After the friction of their initial meeting she had treated him with impersonal politeness, and he was responding in kind, but all the while he was intensely aware of her presence. It was an odd radar-like, three-dimensional kind of perception which meant that even when he was not looking at Prudence he knew exactly where she was and what she was doing. This invasion of his mind was troublesome and disturbing, and when he found that it extended to minutiae like the design of her jacket buttons and the pattern of stitching in her boots his sense of aggravation increased. He slumped in the spacious darkness of the rear seat of the car Ambrose had rented that afternoon and thought nostalgically about other girls he had known. There had, for instance, been Eva—the German interpreter in Malaq—who understood the principle of sexual *quid pro quo*. That had been less than three years earlier, but Snook was annoyed to find he could no longer remember Eva's face.

". . . have to give the planet a name," Ambrose was saying

in the front seat. "It has always been, literally, an underworld, but it doesn't seem right to call it Hades."

"Gehenna would be worse," Prudence replied. "And there's Tartarus, but I think that was even further down than Hades."

"It hardly fits, under the circumstances. From what Gil says about the levels in the mine, the anti-neutrino world will have completely emerged from the Earth in about seventy years." Ambrose swerved to avoid a pothole and roadside trees were momentarily doused with light from the headlamps. "That's if it continues separating at the same rate, of course. We don't know for sure that it will."

"I've got it." Prudence moved closer to Ambrose, and Snook—watchful in his dark isolation—knew she had clutched his arm. "Avernus!"

"Avernus? Never heard of it."

"All I know is that it was another one of those mythological underworlds, but it's much more euphonious than Hades. Don't you think it sounds quite pastoral?"

"Could be," Ambrose said. "Right! You've just christened your first planet."

"Do I get to break a bottle of champagne over it? I've always wanted to do that."

Ambrose laughed appreciatively and Snook's gloom deepened. The situation at the mine was tense and dangerous, one in which he felt the need to have the big battalions behind him, and he was heading back into it accompanied by what seemed to be the world's last example of the squire-scientist and his new girl friend. There was also the possibility of having to listen to their small-talk right through the night, a prospect he found unbearable. Snook began to whistle, quite loudly, choosing an old standard he had always liked for its sadness, *Plaisir d'amour*. Prudence allowed him to complete only a few bars then leaned forward and switched on the radio. The strains of a heavily orchestrated version of the same song filled the car.

Ambrose half-turned in the driving seat. "How did you do that?" he said over his shoulder.

"Do what?"

"You began to whistle a tune and then we got the same one on the radio." Ambrose was obviously intrigued. "Do you have an ear set?"

"No. I just started to whistle." Snook failed to see why the other man should be so interested in a trivial occurrence which, while not common in his own experience, was not exceptionally rare either.

"Have you thought of the odds against that happening?"

"They can't be too high," Snook said. "It happens to me every now and again."

"The odds are pretty fantastic—I know some people in ESP research who would love to get their hands on you." Ambrose began to sound excited. "Have you ever considered that you might be telepathic?"

"On radio frequencies?" Snook said sourly, wondering if he should revise his estimate of Ambrose's standing in the scientific world. He had gleaned that the man had a doctorate in nuclear physics and was director of a planetarium—qualifications which, Snook belatedly realised, were strangely incompatible and no guarantee that he was not dealing with a plausible crank.

"Not on radio frequencies—that wouldn't work," Ambrose replied. "But if thousands of people all around you were listening to a tune on their radios, you might pick it up directly from their brains."

"I usually live where there's nobody around me." Snook began to have doubts about Ambrose's whole concept of an anti-neutrino universe. Back in the hotel, with the gin glowing in his stomach, and in the verbal high tide of Ambrose's enthusiasm, it had all seemed perfectly logical and natural, but . . .

"Do you get any other indications?" Ambrose was unabashed. "Premonitions, for example. Do you ever get a feeling that something's going to happen before it actually does?"

"I . . ." The question caused upheavals in Snook's subconscious.

Prudence came in, unexpectedly. "I once read about a man who could hear radio broadcasts because he had metallic fillings in his teeth."

Snook laughed gratefully. "Some of my back teeth are like steel bollards," he lied.

"All kinds of effects can crop up if somebody is close to a powerful radio transmitter," Ambrose persisted, "but that's got nothing to do with . . ." He paused as the music on the radio was cut off by the strident chimes of a station announcement.

"We interrupt this programme," an urgent male voice said, "because reports are coming in of a serious incident on the border between Barandi and Kenya, near the main road from Kisumu to Nakuru. It is reported that fighting has flared up between the Barandian Defence Forces and a unit of the Kenyan Army which had crossed into Barandian territory. A communiqué from the Presidential office states that the intruders have been repulsed with heavy casualties, and there is no danger to Barandian civilians. We will bring you further reports as they become available. This is the National Radio Corporation of Barandi serving all its citizens, everywhere."

The chimes sounded again and the music returned.

"What does that mean, Gil?" Ambrose looked out through the side windows as though expecting to see bomb flashes. "Are we going to be mixed up in a war?"

"No. It sounds like another exercise by Freeborn's Mounted Foot." Snook went on to tell what he knew about Barandi's military organisations, ending with a brief character sketch of Colonel Tommy Freeborn.

"Oh well, you know what they say," Ambrose commented. "Inside every nut there's a colonel trying to get out."

"I like that." Prudence laughed and moved even closer to Ambrose. "This trip is turning out to be more fun than I expected."

Snook squirmed in the rear seat, lit a cigarette and thought dismal thoughts about the difficulties of remaining in control of one's own life. In this case, he could pinpoint the exact moment at which things had begun to slip from his grasp—it was when he had yielded to moral pressure from George Murphy and agreed to see the hysterical miner. Since then he had become more and more entangled. It was high time for the human neutrino to slip away, to regain his remoteness in a new phase of life in a distant place, but the bonds had grown strong. He had allowed himself to interact with other human particles, and it now seemed likely that he had strayed inside the radius of capture . . .

When they reached Snook's bungalow the car lights showed three men sitting on the front steps. Remembering his visit from the soldiers in the morning, Snook got out of the car first. He was relieved to see that one of the men was George Murphy, although the other two were strangers. They were boyish-looking Caucasians, both with sandy moustaches. Murphy came forward, smiling and handsome in his silvercords, and waved a heavily bandaged hand.

"Gil," he said happily, "I'll never know how you did it."

"Did what?"

"Got this scientific commission set up. Alain Cartier called me and said the mine was officially closed until an investigation had been completed. I've to co-operate with you and the team."

"Oh, yes—the team." Snook glanced at the car in which Ambrose and Prudence were busy gathering up possessions. "We haven't exactly got a Manhattan Project going here."

Murphy looked in the same direction. "Is that all there is?"

"That's all, so far. As far as I can make out there was quite a bit of Press interest in our ghosts, but the way Helig's story was handled mustn't have impressed many scientific bodies. Who have you got here?"

"Two kids from the electronics plant—Benny and Des, they call themselves. They're so keen to see the ghosts that they came out from town on a motorbike this afternoon. It was right after I spoke to Cartier so I told them to hang around until you got back. Do you think they'll be able to help?"

"That's something for Doctor Ambrose to decide," Snook said sombrely, "but, if you ask me, we're going to need all the help we can get."

As Snook would have predicted, Prudence Devonald avoided even setting foot in his kitchen, and so he spent the next few hours making coffee on an almost continuous basis. Between times, he watched carefully as Ambrose explained his theory to Murphy, Benny Culver and Des Quig. The young men, it turned out, were New Zealanders with good electronic engineering qualifications. They had been attracted to Barandi by the high salaries offered in the electronics plant which President Ogilvie had set up four years earlier in an attempt to broaden the country's economy. Snook got the impression they were clever individuals and he was interested to note that, after a period of free-wheeling discussion, both completely accepted Ambrose's ideas and became feverishly enthusiastic.

George Murphy was no less convinced, and at Ambrose's request went off to his office to fetch layout charts of the mine workings. When he returned, Ambrose taped the charts to a wall, questioned Murphy closely about the exact positions of the sightings, and drew two horizontal lines across the sectional view. He measured the distance between the lines, then drew others above them at equal spacings. The eighth line lay just above ground level.

"The bottom line is approximately the level the Avernians rose to on the morning the first one was seen by the miner, Harper," Ambrose said. "The next one up shows roughly the level they reached on the following morning when Gil took his photographs, and the scale of the chart indicates there was an increase of just over five hundred metres. Assuming a constant rate of separation between Avernus and Earth, we can predict the levels they will attain on successive days. Two days have passed since the last sighting, which means that around dawn this morning we can expect the Avernians to reach here." Ambrose touched the fifth line from the bottom, one which ran through an area in which extensive tunnelling was indicated.

"We could wait for them at any of the lower levels, of

course, but the geometry involved means that when they reach the highest point there is a period when they almost stop moving vertically with reference to us. I see from the chart that, luckily, there has been a lot of excavation around that level. What we have to do is spread out laterally as much as possible—probably just one person to a tunnel—and look for buildings materialising. We're not so much interested in the Avernians themselves at this stage, but we do want to find buildings."

"I seem to have missed something," Snook said, setting down a pot of fresh coffee. "Why are buildings so important?"

"They represent our best chance of establishing contact with the Avernians, and even then it may not work. The only reason we were able to detect them is that a mine is a pretty dark place, and so the conditions were good for seeing ghosts. In daylight they might never have been noticed."

"We were able to see Thornton's Planet in daylight," Culver said.

Ambrose nodded. "True—but in its own universe Thornton's Planet is a very dense assembly of anti-neutrinos and is emitting neutrinos in four-pi space at a very high rate. The planet Avernus is less dense, in its own universe, and therefore its surface appears to us as the milky luminance which Gil and George described. The *inhabitants* of Avernus are less dense again—just the way my hand is a lot less solid than a steel bar—so their neutrino flux is even more attenuated, and they are therefore much harder to see. Okay?"

"I think I get it, but does that explain the way the Avernians were seen gradually emerging bit by bit from the floor? If we see them by virtue of their neutrino emission shouldn't they be more or less visible all the time? Shouldn't we see them right through the solid rock?"

"No. Not to any important extent anyway. The neutrino flux decreases according to the inverse square law, and if you start off with a weak emitter, like an Avernian being, the flux soon attenuates to below the threshold level at which the Amplites will produce an image. The glasses aren't a very efficient way of seeing the Avernian universe—at best they leave us desperately short-sighted."

"But they're super-efficient in this universe," Quig put in. "Even in the dark they would give you a good image of the floor and that could blot out faint images of what was below the floor."

"Correct." Ambrose nodded his agreement. "It's a bit like not being able to see stars in the daytime sky, even though they're there just the same."

"And the reason we're hoping to find structures," he continued for Snook's benefit, "is that it might be dark inside an Avernian building, and that would give them a better chance to see us. Don't forget that, as far as they're concerned, *we* are the ghosts. Right now, sitting in this room, we're sailing along in their atmosphere. The rotation of the two planets means that we're on a kind of glide path which will intersect with their equivalent of Barandi just before dawn."

Prudence raised her head. "Is it night time in Avernus?"

"In this hemisphere, yes."

"Then maybe they know about us. Perhaps they can look up in the sky and see us."

"No. If you look at the two circles again you'll notice that the Avernians are under the surface of the Earth, so all they would see, if they see anything, is a general radiance—as happened when Gil and George sank under their surface. The only time we can communicate with them is when the two surfaces are roughly coincident."

"Hell! I've just thought of something which wrecks the whole plan," Culver put in, slapping his forehead. "We would never have detected the Avernians at all if our miners hadn't been wearing magniluct glasses. So the Avernians would need special viewing aids to see us, wouldn't they. And the chances that they'd just happen to be wearing them are bound to be millions to one against."

"Good point." Ambrose smiled at Culver, obviously pleased at the question having arisen. "But, fortunately, the relationship between the two universes is not symmetrical, and the advantage is on our side. What it boils down to is that we are better emitters than they are. I've done a few sums and it looks to me that if we stand in an intermediate vector boson field it will have the effect of making us glow fairly strongly in their universe."

"Bosons? That's a funny kind of radiation, isn't it?"

"Yes, but it should be the Avernian equivalent to a shower of photons."

"Will you need a Moncaster machine? Des and I have a friend at the power station who uses one sometimes."

"A lab model would be too big and heavy. I brought some portable equipment with me from the States—it creates a low-intensity field, but it should be good enough for our purpose. I only had room for one so we're going to need good communications in the mine. Anybody who finds what he thinks is an Avernian building will signal the others and we'll get the radiation equipment to him as fast as we can."

Des Quig put up his hand, like a boy in class. "If we need communicator sets I can rig up something at the plant."

"Thanks, but we're too short of time. That's why I brought as much commercially available equipment as I could get in the few hours I had—pulse code modulation sets and . . ."

"Hey! It sounds as if you're planning to talk to the ghosts."

Ambrose looked surprised. "Of course! It's technically feasible, isn't it? If they can see us and we can see them, that means light is being exchanged. All you have to do is modulate it to get sound communication."

"That's assuming the Avernians use speech among themselves, that they are a technical race at the same level as ourselves or more advanced, and that we can get the idea of light-to-sound conversion over to them. And all that's on top of assuming we will even manage to make them see us."

"Correct. I know I'm rushing a lot of fences, and I know that being wrong in any one of the assumptions you mention will wreck the whole scheme, but we've got to make the effort—starting tonight."

Quig burst out laughing. "Where did I get the idea that astronomers were patient, slow-moving types? Why all the hurry?"

"We're hurrying because it was a stroke of pure luck that the Avernians were seen in a deep mine, and it has given us a few days' grace in which to try making contact." Ambrose tapped the sectional chart again.

"Let me remind you of the geometry of the situation. We're dealing with two kinds of movement. One of them is the separation of the two worlds—Avernus is emerging from the Earth at a speed of just over five hundred metres a day. This creates a problem in itself because they rise that much higher each time we see them. At dawn this morning they'll get to about fifteen hundred metres from the surface, tomorrow morning it will be a thousand metres from the surface, the morning after five hundred, and the morning after that they'll be visible on the surface—right out there among the trees and mine buildings, or here in this room." Ambrose paused and smiled as Prudence gave a theatrical shiver.

"That's the stage at which the surface of Avernus coincides with the surface of the Earth—from then on the Avernians will start rising into the sky above us, five hundred metres higher every day, as the planets begin to separate. That would be awkward enough, but the daily rotation of the two worlds complicates everything even further because it is translated into vertical movement between corresponding points on the surfaces of the two spheres."

"That's the bit I'm having trouble with," Murphy confessed, shaking his head.

"Well, you've seen it for yourself. We're standing on the surface of a rotating sphere, the Earth. Just below us is another and slightly smaller rotating sphere which has moved off centre until the surfaces are touching at one side. As the spheres turn, corresponding points will move closer together until they meet at the contact zone, but as the rotation continues they have to move apart again. Twelve hours later, half a day, they'll be at maximum separation, with the inner point far beneath the outer point.

"That's why the Avernians rise up through the floor and sink back down again. The best time to try making contact is when they're at the top of the curve and the downward motion hasn't yet begun. What do you call it when a piston reaches the top of its stroke?"

"Top dead centre," Snook supplied.

"That's when we've got to try to make the first contact with the Avernians—when they're at top dead centre—and that's why there's no time to waste. Tomorrow morning, and for three mornings after that, top dead centre will occur at fairly convenient positions for us—after that it will take place in the air, higher and higher above the mine."

"Four chances," Quig said. "Being strictly realistic about it, Boyce, what can you hope to achieve even if you strike lucky the very first time? Four brief meetings would hardly give the Avernians time to react."

"Oh, we wouldn't be limited to four meetings," Ambrose said airily.

"But you just said . . ."

"I said I was hoping for first contact while top dead centre is in a convenient location, that is, either below ground or on it. After that, when top dead centre is in the air above the mine, we would be able to have quite long meetings."

"For God's sake, how?"

"Think it out for yourself, Des. If you wanted to rise slowly into the air, hover for a while and sink vertically downwards again—what sort of machine would you use?"

Quig's eyes widened. "A helicopter."

"Exactly! I provisionally chartered one today." Ambrose beamed at his audience, like a fond parent surprising his children with an extravagant gift. "Now that we've got that out of the way, let's discuss the immediate problems for a while."

Listening to the conversation, Snook once again began to revise his opinions of Boyce Ambrose. The category he had invented for him, playboy scientist, still seemed appropriate—but Ambrose was playing in earnest, like a man who had a definite goal in mind and was determined that nothing would prevent him from reaching it.

Although all work had stopped at the mine, the perimeter fence was still floodlit and the security patrols were in operation. Snook felt vulnerable and selfconscious as he approached the gate, accompanied by George Murphy and the other four members of the group, under the interested stares of the mine guards. He was carrying six squares of heavy cardboard, placards which Ambrose had insisted on making, and they were proving strangely difficult to handle. The night breezes were slight, but even the gentlest puff of air was enough to make the smooth cards twist and slither in his grasp. He began to swear over Cartier's ruling that they could not bring a vehicle into the enclosure.

Murphy, who was well known to the guards, was nevertheless stopped by them and had to produce a letter signed by Cartier before the group were admitted. They straggled through the gate with the various boxes of equipment Ambrose had produced. Prudence remained close to Ambrose, talking quietly to him all the while. This fact produced a fretful resentment in Snook. He explained it to himself by reasoning that she was, if not actually a hindrance, certainly the least useful member of the group and it was therefore inordinate for her to occupy so much of the leader's time. Another level of his mind, one which was immune to deception, regarded this explanation with contempt.

"I see they've taken your advice—too late." Murphy nudged Snook and pointed at new notices, in red lettering, which stated that all below-ground workers were required to hand in their Amplite glasses pending the installation of improved lighting systems in the mine.

"It helps cover up for the closure," Snook said, his attention elsewhere. He had just noticed that two army jeeps were parked in the darkness beyond the gatehouse, each of them containing four men of the Leopard Regiment. As soon as the soldiers saw Prudence they began whooping and jeering. The two drivers switched on spotlights and directed them at Prudence's legs, and one soldier—to the cheers of his comrades—left his vehicle and ran up to her for a close inspection. She walked on calmly, looking straight ahead, holding onto Ambrose's arm. Ambrose, too, ignored the soldier.

Snook took his Amplites from his breast pocket, put them on and looked towards the jeeps. In the blue pseudo-radiance

he saw that a lieutenant, the same one who had been at his
house in the morning, was sitting in one of the vehicles with
his arms folded, unperturbed by the behaviour of his men.

"What do these bastards think they're doing?" Murphy
whispered fiercely, starting towards the nearby soldier.

Snook restrained him. "It isn't our problem, George."

"But that ape needs a kick where it'll do him the most damage."

"Boyce brought her here," Snook said stolidly. "Boyce will
have to look after her."

"What's the matter with you, Gil?" Murphy stared at
Snook, then gave a low chuckle. "I get it. I thought I saw you
doing a bit of quiet mooning in that direction, but I wasn't
sure."

"You saw nothing."

Murphy remained quiet for a moment as the soldier grew
tired of the game and rejoined his comrades. "Was there
nothing doing, Gil? Sometimes those aristocratic types go for
a bit of rough—just for a change, you know."

Snook kept his voice steady. "What's discipline like in the
Leopard Regiment? I thought they were kept on a pretty
tight rein."

"They are." Murphy became thoughtful. "Was there an
officer watching the show?"

"Yes."

"That doesn't have to mean anything."

"I know what it doesn't have to mean."

They reached the mine head and Snook felt his concern
about the behaviour of the soldiers abruptly vanish as it came
to him that, in all probability, he was due for another encounter with the silent, translucent beings who walked in the
depths of the mine. It was all right for Ambrose, who had
never seen the apparitions, to talk knowledgeably about
geometries and planetary movements—facing the reality of
the blue ghosts was another matter entirely. Snook discovered
in himself an intense reluctance to go underground, but he
concealed it as the group assembled at the continuous hoist
and Murphy set the machinery going. The Avernians'
mouths were what he dreaded seeing most, the inhumanly

wide, inhumanly mobile slits which at times seemed to express a sadness beyond his comprehension. It occurred to Snook that Avernus might be an unhappy world, well named after a mythological hell.

"I'll go down first because I know the level we want," Murphy announced. "The hoist moves continuously so you'll have to step off smartly when you see me, but don't worry—it's as easy as using an escalator. If you don't get out in time, stay on until you reach the gallery below, get off there, walk round to the ascending side and come up again. We haven't lost a visitor yet."

The others laughed appreciatively, their spirits recovering from the uneasiness which had been inspired by the near-incident at the gate. They stepped into descending cages two by two, Snook going last with his awkward bundle of cards. His ears popped during the patient, rumbling descent. When he reached the circular landing at Level Three he found Ambrose already holding court, assigning people to the various radial tunnels. The radiation generator, which was the size of a small suitcase, was to be left at the hoist and carried to anyone who shouted that he had found an Avernian building.

"I want everybody to take one of the cards that Gil is holding," Ambrose said. "I know they're a bit of a long shot, but we're playing so many long shots that one more won't make any difference." He took one of the placards and held it up. The design, heavily drawn in black, consisted of three elements—a close-pitched sine wave, and an arrow which pointed from it to another sine wave of much wider pitch.

"This banner with the strange device symbolises the conversion of light to sound." He looked at Quig and Culver. "I think its meaning is quite clear, don't you?"

Quig nodded doubtfully. "Provided the Avernians have eyes and provided they know something about acoustics and provided they have developed a wave theory of light and provided they use electronics and provided . . ."

"Don't go on, Des—I've already admitted that the chances aren't good. But there's so much at stake that I'm prepared to try anything."

"Okay. I don't mind carrying a card," Quig said, "but I'm mainly interested in getting photographs. I think that's the most we can hope for." He tapped the camera which was slung round his neck.

"That's all right—I appreciate any help I can get at this stage." Ambrose glanced at his watch. "There's only about a quarter of an hour to go—the Avernians must already be in the lower levels of the mine—so let's take up our stations. Sound carries well in these tunnels, but the acoustics aren't good, so don't go more than about a hundred metres from the central shaft. Keep wearing your Amplites, turn off all flashlights ten minutes from now, and don't forget to holler at the top of your voice if you find what we're looking for."

There was another general laugh which filled Snook with a perverse malice—he wondered how many of the group would still be amused when, and if, the Avernians kept their appointment. He started for the south pipe, then noticed that Prudence was walking beside him on her way to an adjoining branch. She was carrying a card and a flashlight, but her slim figure and salon clothing were incongruous against the backdrop of rock surfaces and mine machinery. Snook felt an unwanted pang of concern.

"Are you going in there alone?" he said.

"Don't you think I should?" Her face was inscrutable behind the blue lenses of her Amplites.

"Frankly, no."

The curvature of her lips altered. "I didn't see you showing much concern for my safety when your friends were having their bit of fun at the gate."

"*My* friends!" Snook was so taken aback by the unfairness of the remark that he was unable to frame a sentence before Prudence was flitting away along the tunnel. He stared after her, lips moving silently, then went on his separate way, swearing inwardly at his own foolishness for having spoken.

The deposits of diamond-bearing clay had been wide and deep here, and its removal had left the semblance of a natural underground cavern. Parasonic projectors turned rock and clay into dust, without affecting the harder material of diamonds, and they had another advantage in that they did not

split or strain the rock structures, which meant that little
shoring was required. Snook followed the curvature of the
spacious tunnel until he estimated he had gone a hundred
metres, then he stopped and lit a cigarette. A very small
amount of illumination reached this far from the fluorescent
tubes in the main shaft, but his Amplites transformed it into a
visible wall of light which he felt might be strong enough to
screen out any ghosts which appeared. Accordingly, he
turned his back to the light and stood facing the darkest part
of the tunnel. Even then, the glow of his cigarette was almost
unbearably bright when seen through the magniluct glasses.
Snook ground the cigarette out under his foot and stood perfectly still, waiting.

A few minutes went by, like so many hours, then—without
warning—a large glowing bird emerged at speed from the
wall beside his head, flashed silently across his field of view,
and disappeared into the sculpted rock at the far side of the
tunnel. Its image had been faint, but he had the impression
that he had still been able to see it for a second after it entered
the wall, as though the stone itself was becoming lacy and insubstantial.

Snatching for breath, he turned and looked back towards
the main shaft. The wall of bluish light was there as before,
but now it had several darker rectangles in it. Snook frowned,
wondering why he had not noticed the angular patches before, then came the realisation that he was looking at the outline of windows.

"This way!" he shouted, sick with apprehension, yet unable to prevent himself running forward. "South tunnel!
There's something in the south tunnel!"

He headed straight for one of the dim rectangles, hesitated
briefly, and plunged through the vertical barrier of radiance.
An Avernian was standing before him, cradling an indistinct
object in its arms, the complex folds of its robes fluttering
slightly in a breeze which did not exist on Earth. Its eyes ro-
tated slowly near the top of the tufted head, and the wide
mouth was partially open.

"Hurry up," Snook bellowed. "I'm in a room with one of
them!"

"Hold on, Gil," came a reassuring, echoing reply from the distance.

The voice contact with another human being eased the churning in Snook's mind. He made a conscious effort to be observant, and saw that the Avernian seemed taller than the others. He glanced down at its feet and discovered that the horizontal plane of milky blue radiance which was the Avernian's floor was on a level with his own knees. As he watched, the level crept slowly up his thighs. At the rate of movement the ghostly floor would soon be above Snook's head. He looked around the room and picked out shapes that were recognisably furniture, a table and chairs of curious proportions. The Avernian swayed slightly, in a nameless dance, unaware that its privacy was being violated by a watcher from another universe.

"Hurry up, for Christ's sake," Snook shouted. "Where are you, Boyce?"

"Right here." The voice came from close at hand, and Snook saw human figures moving. "The machine was heavier than I thought. Stand still—I'm going to try to light you up for him. There! Now hold the card above your head and move it around."

Snook had forgotten about his placard. The pool of faint luminance had reached his chest, but its rate of climb had decreased. He raised the card above his head, then moved to the side so that he was facing the alien figure.

His eyes looked into the Avernian's. The Avernian's eyes looked into his. And nothing happened.

I'm not real, Snook thought. *I don't exist.*

"This isn't working," he called out to Ambrose. "There's no reaction."

"Don't give up—I'm increasing the field intensity."

"Okay." There was a clicking of cameras in the background.

Snook noticed that the floor level of the other room was beginning to sink down his body again, then it dawned on him that the Avernian had not moved for several seconds, that its eyes were still fixed on him. The wide slash of its mouth writhed.

"I think something might be happening," Snook said.

"Could be." Ambrose had moved until he was standing beside Snook in the extra-dimensional room.

The alien turned abruptly, the first rapid action Snook had seen any of its kind perform, and strode across the floor. It appeared to sit at the table and there were movements of the oddly jointed arms. The translucent floor level continued to fall until it had merged with the rock floor of the tunnel, then the Avernian's webbed feet began to sink into it.

"There isn't much time left," Ambrose said. "I think we were wrong to expect a reaction."

Quig joined them, camera held to his eye. "I'm getting as much as I can on film anyway."

At that moment the Avernian stood up in a slow-flowing movement and turned to face them. Its arms were extended from the pleated robes and in its hands was a faintly visible square of thin material. Due to the translucency of the alien and everything about it, Snook had trouble in discerning that there were marks on the square sheet. He narrowed his eyes and picked out an almost invisible design: tightly-waved lines; an arrow; loosely-waved lines.

"That's our message," Ambrose breathed. "We got through to him. And so *fast!*"

"There's something else there," Snook said. Further down on the faint square was another diagram—two slightly irregular circles almost fully superimposed.

"It's astronomical." Ambrose was hoarse with excitement. "They know what's happening!"

Snook kept staring at the second diagram, and deep in his guts there heaved the iciness of premonition. The symbols of the upper diagram were flawlessly drawn—the sine waves exactly regular, the lines of the arrow dead straight, which suggested the Avernian was a good draughtsman. And yet the two overlapping circles of the lower diagram—which Ambrose supposed to represent two well-nigh perfect spheres—had definite irregularities. They also had several internal markings . . .

The Avernian was now sinking, with its world, below the rock floor of the tunnel.

It came towards Snook, apparently wading knee-deep in stone, and reached upwards with webbed translucent hands, the long trembling fingers circling to enclose Snook's head.

"No!" Snook backed off from the yearning hands, unable to prevent himself from shouting. "I'm not doing it. Never!"

He turned and ran towards the main shaft.

CHAPTER EIGHT

"Gil, I don't see why you refuse to accept this thing," Boyce Ambrose said impatiently.

He threw the sheaf of photographs down on the table. "When we were driving out here—only hours after having met you—I suggested you were telepathic. That sort of thing is an established and respectable scientific phenomenon these days. Why won't you admit it?"

"Why do you want me to admit it?" Snook spoke in a sleepy voice, nursing his drink.

"I mean the fact that you understood the Avernian diagram, when I thought it was astronomical, *shows* that you have a telepathic faculty."

"You still haven't said why you're so keen for me to claim this power," Snook persisted.

"Because . . ."

"Go on, Boyce."

"I would do it," Ambrose said, a hint of bitterness in his voice. "I would do it if I had been chosen."

Snook swirled the gin in his glass, creating a miniature vortex. "That's because you've got the scientific spirit, Boyce. You're one of those people who would fly a kite in a thunderstorm, regardless of the danger, but I'm not going to let any blue monster shove its head inside mine."

"The Avernians are people." Prudence eyed Snook with disdain.

Snook shrugged. "All right—I'm not going to let any blue people shove their heads inside mine."

"The idea doesn't bother me."

"That remark just cries out for an obscene reply, but I'm too tired." Snook settled further down in the armchair and closed his eyes, but he had time to see Prudence tighten her lips in anger. *I owed you that one*, he thought, pleased at having scored a point, yet appalled at his own childishness.

"Too drunk, you mean."

Without opening his eyes, Snook raised his glass in Prudence's direction and took another drink. He found he could still see the translucent blue face advancing on his own, and a hard knot formed in his stomach.

"I think," Ambrose said anxiously, "it might be a good idea if we all got some rest. We've been up all night and we're bound to be tired."

"I've got to get back to the plant," Culver said. He turned to Des Quig, who was still examining the pictures he had taken. "How about you, Des? Want a ride back?"

"I'm not going back," Quig replied, absently stroking his sandy moustache. "This is too much fun."

"How about your job?" Ambrose asked. "I appreciate your help here, but . . ."

"They can shove my job. Do you know what they've got me doing? Designing radios, that's what I'm doing." He had been drinking neat gin, while exhausted and hungry, and his voice was beginning to slur. "That would be bad enough, but I design them a *good* radio and they hand it over to the commercial people. You know what happens then? The commercial people start taking bits out of it . . . and they keep doing that till the radio stops working . . . then they put the last bit back in again—and *that's* the radio they put into production. It makes me sick. No, I'm not going back there. I'm damned if I'll . . ."

Recognising a cry from the heart, Snook opened his eyes and saw Quig lay his head on his arms and promptly fall asleep.

"I'll go then," Culver said. "See you tonight." He left Snook's living room and George Murphy went at the same time, saluting tiredly with his bandaged hand.

Snook got to his feet, waving the two men goodbye, and turned to Ambrose. "What do you want to do?"

Ambrose hesitated. "I've had about four hours' sleep in the last three days. I hate to impose, but the thought of driving back to Kisumu . . ."

"You're welcome to stay here," Snook said. "I've got two bedrooms, with one bed in each. Des seems very comfortable at the table, so if I sleep on the couch in here, you and Prudence can have a bedroom each."

Prudence stood up also. "I wouldn't dream of keeping you out of your own bed. I'll go in with Boyce—I'm sure I won't come to much harm."

Ambrose grinned and rubbed his eyes. "The tragedy is that, the way I feel now, you probably won't come to *any* harm." He put an arm around Prudence's shoulders and they walked into the bedroom which was directly across the corridor from the living room. Prudence reappeared in the opening as she closed the door and, in the narrowing aperture, her eyes steadied on Snook's for the briefest instant. He tried to smile, but his lips refused to conform.

Snook went into the other bedroom. The early morning sun was blazing in from the east, so he closed the blind, creating a parchment-coloured dimness. He lay down on the bed without undressing, but the tiredness which had been so insistent a few minutes earlier seemed to have fled his system, and it was a long time before he was able to escape from his loneliness into sleep.

Snook was awakened in the late afternoon by the sound of a loud, unfamiliar voice filtering through from his living room. He got up, ran his fingers through his hair and went to see who the visitor was. He found Gene Helig, the Press Association representative, standing in the centre of the room and talking to Ambrose, Prudence and Quig. Helig, who was a lean, greying Englishman with drooping eyelids, gave Snook a critical glance.

"You look bloody awful, Gil," he said heartily. "I've never seen you look so bad."

"Thanks." Snook sought a parry to Helig's remarks but the pounding in his head made it difficult to think. "I'm going to make some coffee."

Des Quig sprang to his feet. "I've already done it, Gil. Sit down here and I'll fetch you a cup."

Snook nodded gratefully. "Four cups, please. I always have four cups." He dropped into the chair Quig had vacated and looked around the room. Ambrose was regarding him with concerned eyes; Prudence appeared not to have noticed his arrival. Though wearing the same clothes as on the previous day, she was as cream-smooth and immaculate as ever. Snook wondered if, at any time during their hours in bed, Ambrose had succeeded in disturbing that practised serenity.

"You've set the cat among the pigeons this time," Helig boomed. "Do you know a couple of Freeborn's men have been following me around since I filed that story of yours?"

"Please, Gene." Snook pressed his temples. "If you'll speak in normal conversational tones I'll hear you all right."

Helig switched to a penetrating whisper. "That convinced me there was something important in it. I wasn't too sure, you know, and I'm afraid it showed through in the way I wrote the piece."

"Thanks, anyway."

"That's all right." Helig switched to his usual stentorian voice. "It's all different now, of course, what with your ghosts having popped up in Brazil and Sumatra as well."

"What?" Snook glanced at Ambrose for confirmation.

Ambrose nodded. "I said this would happen. It was perhaps a little sooner than I expected, but it doesn't do to regard the Earth's equator as a perfect circle. The whole planet is deformed slightly by tidal forces and, of course, the Earth wobbles in its orbit as it swings around the Earth-Moon barycentre. I don't know how closely Avernus follows that movement, and there could be all kinds of libration effects which . . ." Ambrose stopped speaking as Prudence leaned across to him and pressed a hand to his mouth. The little public intimacy caused Snook to look quickly in another direction, racked with jealousy.

"Sorry," Ambrose concluded. "I tend to get carried away."

"There's a hell of a lot of world interest now," Helig said. "I heard Doctor Ambrose's name mentioned a couple of times this morning on the main satellite networks."

Prudence laughed delightedly, and gave Ambrose a playful push. "Fame at last!"

Snook, still intensely aware of Prudence and everything in her ambit, saw an unreadable expression flicker across Ambrose's face, perhaps a mixture of wistfulness and triumph. It was gone on the instant, to be replaced by Ambrose's customary look of humorous alertness, but Snook felt he had gained an insight into the other man's character. The playboy scientist, it seemed, was hungry for fame. Or respect. The respect of his professional peers.

"Does that mean a lot more people will be coming here?" Quig said, arriving with Snook's coffee.

"I doubt it." Helig spoke with the bored concern of a colonial who has watched the antics of the natives for too many years. "The President's office has cancelled all new visas for an indefinite period because of this spot of bother with Kenya. Besides, all the scientist johnnies have other places to go now. A hell of a sight easier to pop down to Brazil from the States than to come here, eh? Less chance of getting a *panga* up your backside, too." Helig gave a thunderous laugh which reverberated in the cup from which Snook was drinking. Snook closed his eyes, concentrated on the aromatic taste of sanity, and wished Helig would leave.

"How are you getting on here, anyway?" Helig continued, planted solidly in the centre of the room. "If these ghosts really are inhabitants of another world, do you think we'll ever find a way to talk to them?"

Ambrose spoke cautiously. "We were hoping we might have had a lead in that direction, but naturally it's a tricky problem."

Snook looked over the rim of his cup and his eyes met those of Ambrose and Prudence.

Helig peered at the settings of his wrist recorder. "Come on, Doctor—confession is good for the soul."

"It's too soon," Snook said, reaching a decision he was unable to explain to himself. "Come back tomorrow or the day after, and we might have a good story for you."

When Helig had gone, Ambrose followed Snook out to the kitchen where he was brewing more coffee.

"Did you mean what I thought you meant?" Ambrose said quietly.

"I guess so." Snook busied himself with the rinsing out of cups in the sink.

"I'm grateful." Ambrose picked up a cloth and began drying cups in an inexpert manner. "Look, I don't want you to take this the wrong way, but scientific workers get paid like any other workers. Now, I know you had reasons of your own for getting involved in this thing, but I'd be happy to get it on to a proper business footing if you . . ."

"There's one thing you could do for me," Snook interrupted.

"Name it."

"Somewhere in Malaq there's a Canadian passport belonging to me—and I'd like to have it back."

"I think I can arrange that."

"It could cost you quite a bit in what they call commission."

"Don't worry about it. We'll get you out of Barandi somehow." Ambrose, having dried two cups, apparently felt he had contributed enough in that direction and set his cloth aside. "Actually, tomorrow morning's experiment will be nothing like the last one."

"Why's that?"

"I've been looking at the plans and the vertical section through the mine—and where tomorrow's top dead centre occurs there hasn't been any excavation. We'll have to intercept the Avernian coming through exactly the same spot as last time. He'll be ascending fairly quickly at that stage but, if you feel like it, there'll be another chance when he's on the way down again."

Snook began drying the remaining cups. "We're assuming he'll be there, waiting for us . . ."

"It's the smallest assumption we've made yet. That character was *fast*—no human could have responded so quickly and in such a positive manner. It's my guess that we're dealing with a race which is superior to our own in many ways."

"That wouldn't surprise me, but do you really believe I'll get some kind of telepathic message when our brains are occupying the same space?"

Ambrose raised his shoulders. "There's just no way to predict what will happen, Gil. The most probable result, according to our science—orthodox science, that is—is that nothing at all will happen. After all, your brain has occupied the same space as Avernian rock and you didn't get a headache."

"You chose an unfortunate example." Snook pressed two fingertips delicately against a throbbing vein in his temple, as if taking his pulse.

"Why do you drink so much?"

"It helps me to sleep."

"You'd be better with a woman," Ambrose said. "Same result, but the side-effects are all good."

Snook drove a painful vision from his mind, a vision of Prudence cradled in his left arm, her face turned to his. "We were talking about the telepathy experiment—you think nothing will happen?"

"I didn't say that. The trouble is we know so little about the subject. I mean, telepathy between human beings wasn't proved until a few years ago when they finally got round to throwing out those stupid card-guessing routines. A lot of people would say the brain structure, thought processes and language structure of an extra-terrestrial race are bound to be so incompatible with ours that no communication at all could take place, telepathically or any other way."

"But the Avernians aren't extra-terrestrial—they're just the opposite." Snook wrought with unfamiliar concepts. "If they've existed a few hundred kilometres under our feet for millions of years, and if telepathy really exists, the link might be already established. There might be something like resonance . . . you know, sympathetic resonance . . . the Avernians might be responsible for . . ."

"Common elements in religions? Plutonic mythologies?

The universal idea that hell is under the ground?" Ambrose shook his head. "You're going way beyond the scope of the investigation, Gil, and I wouldn't recommend it. Don't forget that, even though the Avernians do exist inside the Earth, in many respects they're further away from us than Sirius. The most distant star you can see in the sky is at least part of our own universe."

"But you still think the experiment is worth trying?"

Ambrose nodded. "It's got one thing going for it that I can't ignore."

"What's that?" Snook paused in his chores to concentrate on Ambrose's answer.

"The Avernian himself seemed to think it would work."

When the party set out for the mine in pre-dawn blackness, Snook noticed that Prudence had remained behind in his bungalow, and it intrigued him that neither she nor Ambrose had made reference to this fact. They had driven into Kisumu in the afternoon for a meal and a change of clothing at their hotel, and had returned looking like newly-weds. Since then there had been lots of time for discussion of the various arrangements, and yet Prudence's non-participation had not been mentioned, in Snook's presence anyway. It could have been a common-sense decision to avoid possible trouble with the soldiers at the gate, but Snook suspected she had no wish to take part in an event where he was to be the central figure, especially as she had been openly scornful of his running away the previous time. Snook knew he was being reduced to childishness again, but he was perversely pleased at what was happening because it showed she had singled him out, that there was a continuing personal reaction —even if a negative one.

The four men—Snook, Ambrose, Quig and Culver—were met at the enclosure gate by George Murphy, who was already talking to the guards. Murphy came forward to meet the group.

"I don't want any more days like yesterday," he said. "I'm just about wrecked."

"You look okay to me." Snook had never seen Murphy look more assured and indomitable, and he drew comfort from the big man's presence. "What's been happening to you?"

"Been sitting in on arguments. Cartier keeps telling the workface crews that the ghosts don't exist because they can't see them any more, and that they weren't ghosts anyway. The miners keep telling him they know a ghost when they see one, and even when they can't see them they can feel them. I think Colonel Freeborn is turning up the pressure on Cartier."

Snook fell into step close beside Murphy as they were passing through the gate and spoke to him quietly. "I think he's turning up the pressure on everybody. You know, this thing isn't working out the way we hoped it would."

"I know that, Gil. But thanks for doing what you're doing."

"Isn't there any way you could convince the miners that the Avernians can't do them any harm?"

Murphy remained silent for a moment. "You're convinced, but . . ."

"But I ran. Point taken, George."

As they reached the dimness beyond the gatehouse Snook saw two fully-manned jeeps parked in the same place as before. He put on his Amplites, creating for himself a bluish radiance in which he was able to identify the same haughty young lieutenant he had already encountered. The lieutenant's eyes were hidden by his Amplites, standard issue for soldiers on night duties, but his sculpted ebony face gave an impression of fierce watchfulness. It was a look which caused the old stirrings far back in Snook's mind.

"The lieutenant over there," he said. "Is he related to the Colonel?"

Murphy slipped his own magniluct glasses on. "Nephew. That's Curt Freeborn. Stay out of his way. If possible, never even speak to him."

"Oh, Christ," Snook sighed, "not another one."

At the same moment the jeeps' engines roared into life and the spotlight beams lanced through the group of walkers, streaming them with long shadows. The two vehicles rolled forward and began slowly circling the group, sometimes coming so close that one or more of the men had to give way. With the exception of the young lieutenant, the soldiers in the jeeps grinned hugely throughout the manoeuvres. None of them made any sound.

"Those are open vehicles," Murphy said. "You and I could easily yank the drivers out."

"You and I could easily get shot. It isn't worth it, George." Snook kept walking steadily towards the mine head and eventually the jeeps pulled back to their former positions. The group reached the sodium-lit hoist shed and Ambrose set his radiation generator down with a thud.

"First thing in the morning," he said indignantly, "I'm going to report that harassment to the authorities. I'm running out of patience with those bastards."

"Let's get underground," Snook said, exchanging glances with Murphy, "to the devil we don't know."

"And I told you that's the wrong sort of thinking." Ambrose picked up his black box and led the way to the hoist.

The cavern-like tunnel of Level Three did not unnerve Snook as much as he had expected, mainly because he felt himself part of a group which was acting in concert. Ambrose stalked about purposefully, examining luminous crayon marks he had made on the rock floor, setting up his machine, and flicking his fingers over a pocket computer. Culver occupied himself with the pulse code modulator, and Quig with cameras and magniluct filters, while Murphy pottered about clearing small pieces of debris away from the scene of expected action. Snook began to feel unnecessary, helpless.

"About ten minutes to go," Ambrose said to Snook, looking up from his computer. "Now remember, Gil, you're not being pressurised in any way. This is actually just an auxiliary experiment—I'm pinning my faith on the pulse code modulator—so just take it as far as you feel you are able. Okay?"

"Okay."

"Right. Keep on the look-out for some sort of roof structure coming up into view. From what you told us, you missed that yesterday, and it will give a good advance warning." Ambrose raised his voice, beginning to sound happy again. "If you have time, make sketches on the pads I gave you. The design of a roof will also tell us things about the Avernians themselves—say, whether they have rain or not—so everybody keep their eyes open for details."

Leaning against the tunnel wall and watching the final preparations, Snook took out his cigarettes only to have Ambrose give a warning shake of his head. He put the pack away resignedly, wishing he was in another part of the world, doing something else. For instance, lying in a peaceful room, in parchment-coloured shade, with Prudence Devonald's head cradled in his arm, the left arm—as decreed in the Song of Solomon, Chapters Two and Eight, so that his right hand would be free to touch . . .

A luminous blue line began to appear on the rock floor of the tunnel. Within seconds it had risen to become a triangular ridge and Snook, chilled to the core, moved to his designated place. The floor was strangely transparent.

He was so intent on the materialisation that he scarely noticed George Murphy at his side. Murphy's large dry hand sought his and slid into it a tiny whitish object which felt as though it was made of polished ivory.

"Take this," Murphy whispered. "It might help."

Snook was baffled, mind-numbed. "What is it? An amulet?"

"I'm not a bloody savage." Murphy's voice was amiably aggrieved. "It's chewing gum!"

He retreated to the sidelines as a faintly glowing roof structure gradually emerged from the solid rock, looking surprisingly Earth-like in its arrangement of rafters and ties. Snook put the gum into his mouth and was grateful for its commonplace minty warmth as he found himself sinking into a vaguely seen square room where three Avernians waited for him, slit mouths curving and contorting. Two of the translucent beings carried oblong machines, and suddenly there were noises—sad, mewling, alien noises—coming from the direction of the corresponding machine held by Culver. A

human voice sounded too, but Snook was unable to identify
the speaker, nor to comprehend the words, because the third
Avernian was coming towards him with its arms outstretched.

I can't take this, Snook thought in pure panic. *It's too
much.*

The taste of the chicle grew strong in his mouth, a reminder that he was not alone in his ordeal, and—as the floor
levels merged—he obediently stepped towards the Avernian.

The insubstantial face drew near his own, the mist-pools of
the eyes growing larger. Snook inclined his head forward,
yielding himself. There was a merging.

Snook grunted with surprise as his identity was . . . *lost.*

Deep peace of the running wave.

*I am Felleth. My function in society is that of Responder—
which means that I give advice to others, tell them what to do
or what should be done next. No, your concept of the oracle
is incorrect, my function reversed. An oracle would give
forewarning of events, and leave its audience to devise their
own—perhaps incorrect—responses. As the concept of prediction is invalid when one goes beyond the causality of the
growing seed reaching maturation or the falling stone reaching the ground, it is necessary only to appreciate the
significance of what has already occurred and to give infalli-
ble advice on how to react . . .*

*Oracle. Logic arrow pointing to related concept. The stars
foretell. True as the stars above. Astra. Dis-astra.*

Disaster!

Wait, wait, wait! I am in pain.

*The stars in their courses. Planets? Plural? Cyclic? What is
a year?*

*No! Your concept of time is incorrect. Time is a straight
thread, tightly drawn between the Past Infinity and the Future Infinity, light and dark strands—night and day—appearing to alternate, but each is continuous. Continuous, but
twisted . . .*

Wait! The pain increases.

Sun, the provider of day. Planets, ellipses, axial spin. No cloud-roof. Clear skies, many suns. Logic arrow pointing to related concept. Particles, anti-particles. Correct—our relationship almost precisely defined—but there is something else. Anti-particle planet, seen beyond the cloud-roof. In the year 1993 . . .

Confusion of concepts. It is not possible to measure time in any way other than minus-now or plus-now. And yet . . .

One thousand days ago the weight of our oceans decreased. The waters rose into the sky, until they touched the cloud-roof. Then they swept away the People. And the houses of the People . . .

You say I should have known. That I should have been able to predict.

You say . . .

NO!

The minty warmth on Snook's tongue became real again. He found himself kneeling on hard rock, in the midst of anxious faces, his body being steadied by several hands. His Amplites were gone and somebody had switched on a portable light, bringing the tool-marked contours of the tunnel walls into sharp relief and at the same time making them seem stagey and unreal.

"Are you all right, Gil?" Murphy's voice was noncommittal, an indication that he was really concerned.

Snook nodded and got to his feet. "How long was I out?"

"You weren't out," Ambrose said, sternly professorial. "You fell down on your knees. That was when George switched on the light—against my instructions, I might add—and brought the experiment to a premature end by almost blinding us." He turned to Murphy. "You know, George, the instructions with magniluct glasses clearly warn you against switching on a bright light where people are wearing them."

Murphy was unrepentant. "I thought Gil was hurt."

"How could he have been hurt?" Ambrose became businesslike once more. "Oh, well—there's no point in holding a post mortem. We can only hope the few seconds of recordings we did get are worth . . ."

"Just a minute," Snook put in, floundering, still trying to

orient himself in what should have been the familiar universe. "How about Felleth? Did you see how he reacted?"

"Who's Felleth?"

"The Avernian. Felleth. Didn't you . . . ?"

"What are you talking about?" Ambrose's fingers clawed into Snook's shoulders. "What are you saying?"

"I'm trying to find out how long the Avernian's head was . . . you know . . . inside mine."

"Hardly any time at all," Culver said, knuckling his eyes. "I thought I saw him jumping back from you, then George nearly burned my retinas out with his . . ."

"*Quiet!*" Ambrose's voice was almost frantic. "Did it work, Gil? Did you get an impression of the Avernian's name?"

"An impression?" Snook smiled tiredly. "More than that. I was part of his life for a while. That's why I wanted to know how long the contact had been—it seemed like minutes. Perhaps hours."

"What can you remember?"

"It isn't a good place, Boyce. Something went wrong. It's funny, but before we came down here this time I got a kind of idea . . ."

"Gil, I'm going to give you a de-briefing right now and get it on tape while it's still fresh in your memory. Do you feel up to it? Are there any ill effects?"

"I'm a bit shagged out, but it's all right."

"Good." Ambrose held his wrist recorder close to Snook's mouth. "You've already said his name was Felleth—did you get a name for their planet?"

"No. They don't seem to have given it a name. It's the only world they know about, so maybe it doesn't need a name. Anyway, the contact wasn't like that—we didn't have a conversation." Snook began to feel doubts about his ability to give a proper description of the experience, and at the same time something of its enormousness began to dawn on him. An inhabitant of another universe, a ghost, had touched his mind. Lives had mingled . . .

"All right—try going back to the beginning. What is the first thing you remember?"

Snook closed his eyes and said, "Deep peace of the running wave."

"Was that a greeting?"

"I think so—but it seemed more important to him. Their world seems to be mostly water. The wind could take a wave right . . . Oh, I don't know."

"Okay. Skip the greeting—what came next?"

"Felleth calls himself a Responder. That's something like a leader, but he doesn't think of himself as leading. Then there was a kind of argument about oracles and predictions, with him doing all the arguing. He said prediction was impossible."

"An argument? I thought you said you didn't have a conversation."

"We didn't—but he must have had access to my ideas."

"This is important, Gil," Ambrose said briskly. "Do you think he got as much information from you as you got from him?"

"I can't say. It must have been a two-way process, but how could I tell who got the most?"

"Did you get any sense of being pressurised into talking?"

"No. In fact, he seemed to be hurting. There was something about pain."

"Okay. Keep going, Gil."

"He was shocked to learn about stars. They don't seem to have any astronomy. There's a permanent cloud cover—Felleth has it mixed up in his mind with the idea of a roof. He didn't know the relationship between planets and suns."

"Are you certain? Surely they could have devised an astronomy."

"How?" Snook felt oddly defensive.

"It wouldn't be too easy, I know, but there are lots of clues. The cycles of day and night, seasons . . ."

"They don't think that way. Felleth didn't know that his world rotates. He thinks of night and day as being like black and white marks on a straight thread. They don't have seasons. They don't have years. For them, time . . . everything else . . . is linear. They don't have dates or calendars, as we know them. They count time forwards and backwards from the present."

"The system would be too cumbersome," Ambrose stated. "You need fixed points of reference."

"How the hell would you know?" Snook, still shaken, was unable to curb his annoyance at the other man's presumption. "How would you know what way they think? Do you even know how other human beings think?"

"I'm sorry, Gil, but don't get side-tracked—what else can you remember?" Ambrose was unperturbed.

"Well, about the only thing that didn't surprise him was the explanation of the two universes I picked up from you. He said, 'Particles. Anti-particles. Correct. Our relationship almost precisely defined'."

"This is interesting—nuclear physics, but no astronomy. And he qualified the thing a little? He said it was *almost* precisely defined?"

"Yes. Then there was something about time. And Thornton's Planet came into it . . ." Snook's voice faltered.

"What's wrong?"

"I've just remembered . . . this is where he seemed to get really worked up . . . he said that something had happened a thousand days ago. I remember the figure because of the way it came through. I get the feeling he didn't mean exactly a thousand days—it was like the way we talk about something happening a year ago when we mean eleven or twelve or thirteen months."

"What happened, Gil? Did he mention tides?"

"You knew!" Through his confusion, Snook was yet again aware of having to revise his opinions about Ambrose.

"Tell me what was said." Ambrose had become gentle and persuasive, yet demanding.

"One thousand days ago the weight of our oceans decreased. The waters rose into the sky, until they touched the cloud-roof. Then they swept away the People. And the houses of the People."

"This confirms all of my claims," Ambrose said peacefully. "I'll be known. From now on, I'll be known."

"Who's talking about you?" Snook was baffled and angry as strange fears began to stir within him. "What happened on Avernus?"

"It's quite straightforward. Thornton's Planet is of like material to Avernus, and therefore was able to drag it out of its orbit. The tidal effects would have been severe, of course, and we've already learned that Avernus is a watery world . . ."

Snook pressed his hands to his temples. "Most of them were drowned."

"Naturally."

"But they're real *people!* You don't seem to care."

"It isn't that I don't care, Gil," Ambrose said in a neutral voice. "It's just that there's nothing we can do about it. There's nothing anybody can do to help them."

Something in the way Ambrose spoke intensified the turmoil in Snook's mind. He lurched forward and grabbed the material of Ambrose's jacket. "There's more, isn't there?"

"You're under a strain, Gil." Ambrose did not move or try to break Snook's grip. "Perhaps this isn't a good time to discuss it."

"I want to discuss it. Now."

"All right—we hadn't completed the de-briefing anyway. What happened after the Avernian learned about Thornton's Planet?"

"I don't . . . There was something about predictions, I think. The last thing I remember is Felleth screaming, 'No.' Screaming isn't the right word—there wasn't any sound—but he seemed to be in pain."

"This is fascinating," Ambrose said. "The adaptability and speed of your friend Felleth's brain is . . . well, there's no other word for it . . . super-human. And there's the efficiency of his telepathic communication. We've opened whole new fields of study."

"Why did Felleth scream?"

Ambrose gently disengaged himself from Snook's grip. "I'm trying to tell you, Gil. I'm only guessing, but it's a question of how much he was able to pull out of your mind. You're not interested in astronomy, are you?"

"No."

"But you remember something of what you heard or read

about Thornton's Planet being captured by our sun? And about the orbit it took up?"

"I don't know." Snook tried to calm his mind. "There was something about a precessing orbit . . . and about the planet coming back. In ninety-eight years, wasn't it?"

"Go on. It's important for us to find out if you really do know, at a conscious level, what's going to happen."

Snook thought for a moment, the neural connections were made, and a great sadness descended over him. "The next time Thornton's Planet comes," he said in a dull voice, "they reckon it will pass through the Earth."

"That's correct, Gil. You did have the knowledge."

"But Avernus should be separated from the Earth by that time."

"By a short distance, and that's only if it keeps on separating at its present rate. In any case, it won't make any difference—the miss distance will be so small that the catastrophe will be just as complete as if there was a head-on collision." Ambrose glanced around the silent, watchful group. "The Earth won't be affected, of course."

"Do you think Felleth got all that?" Snook was unable to escape from the lethal fugue which was resounding inside his head. "Do you think that was why he screamed?"

"I'd say that's what happened," Ambrose said, his gaze steady on Snook's face. "You told the Avernian that his world, and everybody on it, will be destroyed in less than a century from now."

CHAPTER NINE

As before, emerging from below ground into the pure pastel light of a new day had the effect of easing the pressure on Snook's mind, enabling him to put a distance between himself and the Avernians.

He filled his lungs with sun-seeded air and felt his body

recover from the curious loss of muscle tone, post-coital in its essence, which had followed his encounter with the alien being. The world, his world, looked hearteningly secure and unchangeable, and it was almost possible to dismiss the notion that—within a matter of hours—another world would begin emerging into the light.

It was wrong, he told himself, to think of Avernus and its people breaking through into the light—because, for them, Earth's yellow sun would not exist. On Avernus there would continue to be the same low cloud-roof, so thick that day brought only a general lessening of the overhead darkness. It was a watery, misty world—a blind world—with its steep-roofed dwellings of russet stone clinging like molluscs to the chain of equatorial islands . . .

The Turner-like vision appeared in Snook's consciousness with such clarity that he knew, on the instant, it had come to him from Felleth. It was an after-image, a residue of the strange mind-to-mind communion which had briefly spanned two universes, two realities. He paused, wondering how much knowledge of Avernus had been implanted within him during the moment of supreme intimacy, and how much information he had yielded in return.

"All right, Gil?" Ambrose said, eyeing Snook with proprietory concern.

"I'm fine." The desire to escape being used like a laboratory animal prompted Snook to remain quiet about his new discovery.

"You were looking slightly . . . ah . . . pensive."

"I was wondering about the Avernian universe. You've proved there's an anti-neutrino sun inside our own sun—does that mean it's the same with the other stars in the galaxy?"

"There isn't enough evidence available to support even an educated guess. There's a thing called the Principle of Mediocrity which states that the local conditions in our Solar System must be regarded as being universal, and that—because there's an anti-neutrino sun congruent with Sol—the other stars in the galaxy are likely to have them as well. It's only a principle, though, and I've no idea what the average density of matter in the Avernian universe might be. For all we know

there might be only a handful of their suns scattered around
our galaxy."

"Barely enough to make a wreath."

"A wreath?" Ambrose looked puzzled.

"The Avernians are going to die, aren't they?"

Ambrose lowered his voice in warning. "Don't get person-
ally involved, Gil—it's asking for trouble."

The irony of hearing his own life-long creed from the lips
of a stranger—and in circumstances which had so fully demonstrated its value—appealed to Snook. He gave a dry laugh,
pretended not to notice Ambrose's worried stare, and walked
towards the gate. As he had expected, two jeeps were parked
in the lee of the gatehouse, but there had been a change of
crews and the group passed without any reaction. They were
almost out of sight, around a corner of the building, when an
empty bottle shattered on the ground behind them, sending
transparent fragments scuttling through the dust like glassy
insects. A soldier in one of the jeeps gave a derisive hyena
call.

"Don't worry—I'm making a note of all these incidents,"
Ambrose said. "A few of these gorillas are going to feel sorry
for themselves."

They went out through the gates, Murphy doing the
obligatory talking with the security guards, and turned left
up the slight incline which led to Snook's bungalow. The
wooden dwellings and stores of the small mining community
were deceptively quiet, but there were too many men standing at the street corners. Some of them called greetings to
Snook and Murphy as the group went by, but their very
cheerfulness was an indication of the tension which was gathering in the air.

Snook moved in beside Murphy and said, "I'm surprised so
many people are still here."

"They haven't much choice," Murphy replied. "The
Leopards are patrolling all the exit roads."

At the bungalow Snook went ahead, key in hand, but the
front door was opened before he could reach it and Prudence
came out, looking cool, stylish and inhumanly perfect. She
was wearing an abbreviated blouse held together by a single

knot in the material, and murmured past Snook—in a flurry of silk-slung breasts, blonde hair and expensive perfume—to meet Ambrose. Snook watched jealously as they kissed, keeping his face impassive, and decided not to pass any comment.

"Touching reunion," he heard himself saying, intellectual strategies thrown to the winds. "We must have been away all of two hours." The only discernible effect of his words was that Prudence seemed to press herself more closely to Ambrose's tall frame.

"I've been lonely," she whispered to Ambrose, "and I'm hungry. Let's have breakfast at the hotel."

Ambrose looked uncomfortable. "I was planning to stay here, Prue. There's so much work to be done."

"Can't you do it at the hotel?"

"Not unless Gil goes as well. He's the star of the show now."

"Really?" Prudence looked disbelievingly at Snook. "Well, perhaps . . ."

"I wouldn't dream of going into Kisumu looking like this," he said, touching the black bristles of his crew-cut. Murphy, Quig and Culver exchanged smiles.

"We can eat later," Ambrose said hastily, drawing Prudence into the house. "In fact, a celebration is called for—we made scientific history a little while ago. Just wait till you *hear* this . . ." Still talking enthusiastically he led Prudence into the living room.

Snook went into the kitchen, switched on the coffee machine and splashed his face with cold water at the sink. The homely domesticity of the place made the hopeless grey world of Avernus retreat a little further from his thoughts. He carried a cup of black coffee into the room where the others were discussing the success of the experiment. Culver and Quig were draped across armchairs, in extravagant postures of relaxation, talking about methods of analysing the few Avernian-originated sounds they had recorded. Murphy was standing at a window, chewing thoughtfully and looking out towards the mine.

"We've got coffee or gin," Snook announced. "Help yourselves."

"Nothing for me," Ambrose said. "There's so much to do here that I don't know where to start, but let's try running over Gil's tape." He took off his wrist recorder, adjusted its controls and set the tiny machine inside its amplifier unit.

"Now, Gil, listen carefully and see if this triggers off any other memories. We're dealing with a new form of communication here and we don't know yet how to make the best use of it. I still think pulse code modulation is the best avenue of approach for general communication with the Avernians, but with your help we may be able to learn their language in days instead of weeks or months." He set the machine going and Snook's recorded voice filled the room.

"*Deep peace of the running wave.*"

Prudence, who was sitting on the arm of Ambrose's chair, burst out laughing. "I'm sorry," she said, "but this is ridiculous. It's just too much."

Ambrose silenced the machine and looked up at her in startled reproach. "Please, Prue—this is important."

She shook her head and dabbed her eyes. "I know, and I'm sorry, but all you seem to have proved is that the Avernians are Celts. And it's so silly."

"What do you mean?"

"'Deep peace of the running wave'—it's the first line of a traditional Celtic blessing."

"Are you certain?"

"Positive. My room-mate at college had it pinned to her wardrobe door. 'Deep peace of the running wave to you; Deep peace of the flowing air to you; Deep peace of . . .' I used to know the whole thing by heart." Prudence gave Snook a confident, challenging smile.

"I never heard it before," he said.

"I can't understand this." Ambrose narrowed his eyes at Snook. "Though I suppose it's possible you did hear those words somewhere, long ago, and that they were lying in your subconscious."

"So what? I told you Felleth and I didn't have a conversation. I got ideas from him—and that's the way the first one came over to me."

"It's odd, the coincidence of wording, but there must be an explanation."

"I'll give you one," Prudence said. "Mister Snook found himself with no job, and—being a resourceful sort of a person —he created another one."

Ambrose shook his head. "That isn't fair, Prue."

"Perhaps not, but you're a scientist, Boyce. What real evidence have you got that this wonderful experience was genuine?"

"There's enough internal evidence in Gil's story to satisfy me."

"I don't give a damn whether anybody believes me or not," Snook cut in, "but I repeat that I didn't have an ordinary conversation with Felleth. Some of it came through in words, otherwise I wouldn't have a name for him, but a lot of it was in ideas and feelings and pictures. Avernus is mostly water. There's water right round it, and there's a steady wind, and the Avernians seem to like the idea of waves going continuously round the planet. It seems to signify contentment, or peace, or something like that for them."

Ambrose made a note on a pad. "You didn't mention that before. Not in so much detail, anyway."

"That's the way it works. I might talk for a month and still be remembering extra bits at the end of that time. A while ago I just remembered what their houses look like—not the house we saw a part of, but a general impression of all their houses."

"Go on, Gil."

"They're made of brown stone, and they have long slanted roofs . . ."

"They sound remarkably like ordinary houses to me," Prudence said, smiling again, the slight inward slope of her teeth contriving to make her appear more scornful and aristocratic than ever.

"Why don't you go and . . ." Snook broke off as his mind was flooded with a vivid image of a chain of low islands, each virtually covered with one complex multi-use building rising to a single roof peak in the centre. The images of the island-dwellings were reflected in calm grey seas, creating a series of diamond-shapes, elongated horizontally. One in particular was distinguished by a curious double-span arch, too large to be entirely functional, which perhaps united two natural summits. For a moment the vision was so clear that he could see the darker rectangles of windows, the doors whose sills were lapped by a tideless ocean, the small boats nodding gently at anchor . . .

"This is getting us nowhere." A note of impatience was appearing in Ambrose's voice.

"My feelings precisely." Prudence rose to her feet and directed an imperious stare at Murphy. "I suppose there's an eating place in the village?"

Murphy looked doubtful. "The only place open at this time would be Cullinan House, but I don't think you should go there."

"I'm quite capable of making that sort of decision for myself."

Murphy shrugged and turned away as Snook joined in. "George is right—you shouldn't go there alone."

"Thank you for the show of concern, but I'm also capable of looking after myself." Prudence spun on her heel and left the room. A moment later they heard the front door slamming.

Snook turned to Ambrose. "Boyce, I think you should stop her."

"What's it got to do with me?" Ambrose demanded irritably. "I didn't ask her to attach herself to this group."

"No, but you . . ." Snook decided that a reference to the couple having shared the one bed would reveal too much about his own feelings. "You didn't turn her away."

"Gil, in case you haven't noticed it, Prudence Devonald is an extremely tough, emancipated young woman, and I quite believe her when she says she can look after herself in any company. *For Christ's sake!*" Exasperation pushed Ambrose's voice into the higher ranges. "We've some of the most important scientific work of the century in front of us and all we can do is argue about chaperoning a piece of skirt who wasn't even supposed to be here. Do you think we could at least go through this tape a couple of times? Huh?"

"I've got quite a good shot of the Avernian roof structure here," Quig said placatingly.

Ambrose took the photograph and examined it with determined interest. "Thank you—this will be extremely useful. Now, let's play the tape again and make notes of any questions that occur to us." He activated the tiny machine and sat with one ear turned to it in an exaggerated show of concentration.

Snook prowled around the room, drinking coffee and trying to focus his attention on the strange-sounding tones of his own voice issuing from the recorder. Finally, after about ten minutes, he set his cup down.

"I'm hungry," he said. "I'm going to eat."

Ambrose blinked at him in surprise. "We can have a meal later, Gil."

"I'm hungry now."

Murphy turned away from the window. "I haven't much to do here—I think I'll join you."

"*Bon appetit*," Ambrose said sarcastically, returning his attention to his notes.

Snook nodded and went outside. He and Murphy walked slowly down the hill, ostensibly enjoying the moderate warmth of the air and the flaming colours of the bougainvillaeas, neither man talking very much. They turned into the main street, with its dwindling series of product and agency signs. The quietness and lack of people created a Sunday morning atmosphere. They walked to the corner of the side-street in which Cullinan House was situated. As Snook had almost expected, there was a jeep parked outside the building. He exchanged glances with Murphy and, trying not to shed their air of casualness, they began to walk faster. They reached the dusty shade of the entrance and found a young Asian, who was wearing a barman's white apron, sitting on a beer keg and smoking a cheroot.

"Where's the girl?" Snook said.

"In there." The youth spoke nervously, indicating a doorway on the left. "But you better not go in."

Snook pushed the door open and there was an instant of heightened perception in which his eyes took in every detail of the scene inside. The square room had a bar along the innermost wall and the rest of the floor area was taken up by small circular tables and cane chairs. Two soldiers were leaning on the counter holding beer glasses, their Uzi submachine guns beside them on bar stools. One of the tables had been laid for breakfast and Prudence was standing at it, her arms pinned behind her by a third soldier, a corporal. Lieutenant Curt Freeborn was standing close to the girl, and he froze for a moment—in the act of opening the central knot which held her blouse together—as Snook walked into the room with Murphy close behind him.

"Prudence!" Snook's voice was gently reproachful. "You've started without us."

He kept walking towards the table, aware that the soldiers at the bar were picking up their weapons, but relying on the mildness of his manner to prevent them from taking any hasty action. Freeborn glanced at the door and windows, and his face relaxed into a smile as he realised Snook and Murphy were alone. He returned his attention to Prudence and, with deliberate slowness, finished undoing the silken knot. The material slid aside to reveal her breasts, cupped in chocolate-coloured lace. Prudence's face was pale, immobile.

"Your friend and I have met before," Freeborn said to Prudence. "He likes the funny remarks." His voice was abstracted, like that of a dentist who is making conversation to soothe a patient. He put his hands to Prudence's shoulders and began stripping the blouse downwards, his eyes intent, cool and professional.

Snook examined the breakfast table and saw that nothing on it even remotely resembled a weapon—even the knives and forks were plastic. He moved closer to the table, wishing Prudence could have been spared the degradation she was undergoing.

"Lieutenant," he said unemotionally, "I won't allow you to do this."

"The remarks get funnier." Freeborn took a brassiere strap between forefinger and thumb and drew it down over the curve of Prudence's shoulder. The corporal holding her smiled in anticipation.

Murphy took a step forward. "Your uncle won't see anything funny in this."

Freeborn's gaze flicked sideways at him. "I'll deal with you later, trash."

During the moment of distraction Snook leapt forward, driving himself high into the air, looped his left arm around Freeborn's neck, and when he hit the floor again he had the Lieutenant doubled over in a secure headlock. The soldiers at the bar started forward, both priming their guns. Snook reached sideways with his right hand, took a fork from the table and rammed its blunt tines into the side of Freeborn's startled, upturned eye. He pushed it far enough into the eye socket to cause pain without inflicting severe injury. Freeborn gave a powerful upward surge, trying to lift him off the floor.

"Don't struggle, Lieutenant," Snook warned, "or I'll take your eye out like a scoop of ice cream."

Freeborn gave a cry of mingled pain and outrage as Snook reinforced his words with extra pressure on the fork. The corporal pushed Prudence to one side and the soldiers began kicking tables out of their way as they advanced.

"And tell your gooks to lay down their guns and back off," Snook commanded.

One of the soldiers, his eyes bulging whitely, raised his gun and carefully sighted at Snook's head. Snook twisted the fork a little and felt the warmth of blood on his fingers.

"Stay back, you fools!" Freeborn's voice was hysterical with panic. "Do as he says!"

The two soldiers set the stubby weapons on the floor and backed away, the corporal joining them. Freeborn's hands fluttered imploring against the backs of Snook's legs, like huge anxious moths.

"Lie down behind the bar," Snook said to the retreating men.

Murphy picked up one of the discarded guns. "Gil, there's a liquor storeroom behind the bar."

"That's even better. We'll need the keys to the jeep, as well." Snook turned to Prudence who was re-tying her blouse with trembling hands. "If you'd like to go outside, we'll be with you in a minute."

She nodded without speaking and ran towards the exit. Still maintaining the fierce grip of his arm on Freeborn's neck, and keeping the fork in place, Snook led the lieutenant to the storeroom. Murphy had just finished bundling the three soldiers into the cramped space. He was carrying the machine gun with an unconscious ease which suggested he had experience with similar weapons. Freeborn was forced to shamble like an ape as Snook brought him behind the bar and backed him into the store with his men.

"We'd better have this, Gil." Murphy opened the flap of Freeborn's holster and took the automatic pistol from it. Freeborn was swearing under his breath in a kind of rhythmic chant as Snook gave him a final shove and slammed the heavy door. Murphy turned the key, flipped it into a far corner of the room, ran out from behind the counter and gathered up the two remaining submachine guns.

"Do we want those?" Snook said doubtfully.

"We need them."

Snook clambered over the bar and joined Murphy. "Won't it change things if we steal Army weapons? I mean, up to now all we've done is defend Prudence from gang rape."

"It wouldn't matter if we'd been defending the Virgin Mary." Murphy smiled briefly over his shoulder as he led the way out to the jeep, past the watchful barman. "I thought you knew this country, Gil. The only thing which will keep us safe—for a little while, anyway—is that Junior Freeborn daren't go to his uncle and report that he and three Leopards were tackled and disarmed in a public place by one unarmed white man. The loss of the weapons makes the humiliation complete, because it's the most shameful thing a Leopard can do."

Murphy threw the guns into the jeep's rear seat and climbed in after them. Snook squirmed into the driving seat, beside Prudence, and got the vehicle into motion.

"Another thing is that the colonel is a black racialist. He's even been known to criticise the President for occasionally preferring a white girl—so young Curt will be treading on eggs for a while."

Snook swung the jeep into the main street. "You mean he won't take any action over this?"

"Grow up! All I mean is that the action won't be official." Murphy looked around him with the air of a general considering tactics. "We should leave the jeep here, so there'll be no reason for any of the military to go near your house. I'll put the guns under the back seat."

"Right." Snook brought the vehicle to a halt and they got out, ignoring the curious stares of the few passers-by.

Prudence, who had not spoken once during the whole encounter, was still pale, though she seemed to have recovered her composure. Snook tried to think of something to say to her, but was unable to find a sufficiently neutral form of words. As they were crossing the main street a sports car sliced past them, being driven too fast, and Snook instinctively caught Prudence's arm. He expected her to snatch it away, but to his surprise she sagged against him until he was supporting most of her weight. They crossed the road in that manner and he steered her into the entrance of an empty store, where she leaned against the wall and began to sob. The sound was painful to Snook.

"Come on," he said awkwardly, "I thought you were supposed to be a tough character."

"It was horrible." She tilted her head back against the postered wood, rolling it from side to side, and he saw the clear lacquer of tears on her cheeks. "That lieutenant . . . he was only a boy . . . but he left me with *nothing* . . ."

Snook gazed helplessly at Murphy. "I think we all need a drink."

"I was being dissected," she whimpered. "Pinned out and dissected."

"I've got coffee or gin," Snook said in a matter-of-fact voice. "In your case I would recommend the gin. What do you say, George?"

"The gin is very good," Murphy responded in similar tones. "Gil should know—he practically lives on it."

Prudence opened her eyes and looked at both men as

though seeing them for the first time. "I thought you were going to be killed. You *could* have been killed."

"Nonsense!" Murphy's brown face was incredulous. "What nobody back there realised was that plastic forks are only a part of Gil's armament."

"Really?"

Murphy lowered his voice. "He carries a stainless steel fork as well—in a special shoulder holster."

Snook nodded. "It used to be the jawbone of an ass, but I couldn't stand the smell."

Prudence began to chuckle, Murphy joined in, Snook gave a shaky laugh, and within seconds they were reeling in the doorway like a trio of drunks, weeping with cathartic laughter as the tension left their bodies. On the way up the hill to the bungalow, still intoxicated with relief and the heady joy that comes with the finding of friends, they made dozens of jokes which had only to contain certain key words like "fork" or "jawbone" to be regarded as wildly hilarious. There were fleeting moments during the walk when Snook felt a sense of dismay over the unnaturalness of their behaviour, but he was determined to remain high for as long as possible.

"I've got to say something before we go in," Prudence said when they reached the bungalow's front steps. "If I don't thank you now it'll get more and more difficult for me. I'm not the easiest of people to . . ."

"Forget it," Snook said. "Let's have that drink."

Prudence shook her head. "Please. I haven't laughed so much in years—and I know why you made me laugh—but it wouldn't have been at all funny if Boyce hadn't sent you after me."

Murphy opened his mouth to speak, but Snook silenced him with a barely perceptible shake of his head.

"We'd better go inside," he said. "Boyce will be glad to see you."

At noon a reduced party—consisting of Snook, Ambrose, Prudence and Quig—drove to the Commodore Hotel in Ki-

sumu for a meal. Ambrose also needed to make some telephone calls there, because it had been discovered that the line
to Snook's house had developed a fault. Prudence was sitting
beside him in the front seat, occasionally leaning her head on
his shoulder. Bright-hued shrubs and trees, many with great
trusses of flowers, streamed past the car's windows like a continuous light show. Snook, who was in the rear seat with
Quig, allowed the varicoloured display to hypnotise him into
a mood of sleepy carelessness in which he was not required to
think too deeply about his situation. Barandi had become a
dangerous place for him and yet, instead of cutting the bonds
and slipping away, he was allowing himself to become even
more deeply enmeshed.

"I don't like the way things are working out here," Ambrose said, echoing Snook's thoughts. "Even without what
you've told me, I can feel a definite hostility in the air. If we
hadn't been so lucky in other respects I'd be tempted to pull
up stakes and go to one of the other countries where the
Avernians have been sighted."

"Is it really worth hanging on here?" Snook said, sitting
upright as his interest kindled. "Why not move on?"

"It's mainly a question of geometry. Avernus is like a
wheel rolling within a wheel at this time, and the point of
contact is constantly moving around its equator. It means that
the Avernians who were sighted in Brazil are a different lot to
the Avernians who appear here—and we've had this fantastic
stroke of luck in getting you together with Felleth. That's the
big attraction in Barandi. That's what has given me the lead
on all the others."

Quig stirred out of his own reveries. "How much more do
you want to find out from him, Boyce?"

"Hah!" Ambrose hunched over the steering wheel and
shook his head in despair. "At the moment all I'm doing is
unlearning."

"I don't get you."

"Well, I haven't discussed this because we've had so many
immediate practical problems to deal with, but the descrip-
tions of Avernus that Gil has given me—even the pictures we
got of the Avernian roof structure—have upset a lot of our

ideas about the nature of matter. According to our physics the Avernian universe should be very weakly bound compared to the one we know. If I'd been asked to describe it a week ago, I'd have said it could exist only because anti-neutrinos have different masses, depending on their energy, and that all objects in that universe would consist of heavy particles surrounded by clouds of lighter particles." Ambrose began to speak faster as he got into his subject.

"This indicates that their compounds wouldn't be formed by electronic forces like electro-valency or covalency. The weakness of the interactions would mean that all bodies in that universe—even the Avernian people themselves—would be a lot more . . . ah . . . statistical than we are."

"Hey!" Quig began to sound excited. "You mean one Avernian should be able to walk right through another Avernian? Or through a wall?"

Ambrose nodded. "That was the old picture, but we've learned that it's all wrong. Gil talked about stone buildings and islands and oceans . . . the rest of us saw those Earth-like roof beams . . . so it appears that an Avernian's world is just as real and hard and solid to him as ours is to us. There's one hell of a lot we have to learn, and Felleth seems to be the best source of information. Felleth teamed up with Gil, that is. That's why I hate the idea of quitting this place."

Snook, who had been listening to the conversation with growing bafflement, suddenly felt that the relationship between Ambrose's world of nuclear theory and his own world of turbines and gearboxes was just as tenuous as that between Earth and Avernus. He had often been surprised at the sorts of things people needed to know in order to function in their jobs, but Ambrose's field of expertise—in which people were treated as mobile clouds of atoms—was cold and inimical to him. Memories began to stir in his mind, half-recollections of something gleaned during his last encounter with Felleth.

He tapped Boyce on the shoulder. "Remember I told you Felleth said, 'Particle, anti-particle—our relationship almost precisely defined'?"

"Yes?"

"I think something else has just come out of it."

"What sort of thing?"

"Well, I don't understand this, but I've got a kind of a picture of the phrase 'particle, anti-particle' representing one edge of a cube, only the cube isn't an ordinary cube. It seems to go off in a lot more directions . . . or maybe each edge of it is a cube in its own right. Does that make any kind of sense?"

"It sounds as though you're wrestling with the concept of multi-dimensional space, Gil."

"What's the point of it?"

"I think," Ambrose said gloomily, "Felleth knows that the relationship between our universe and his is only one of a whole spectrum of such relationships. There may be universe upon universe—and we haven't got the right sort of mathematics to let us even begin thinking about them. Hell, I've *got* to stay in Barandi as long as I can."

Snook's thoughts reverted to the human aspects of the situation. "Okay, but if we're going back to the mine in the morning, I think you should call the Press Association office and round up Gene Helig and force him to go with us. He's the nearest thing we've got to a guarantee of safe conduct."

CHAPTER TEN

They reached the mine head without incident, largely because Murphy had seen Cartier in the afternoon and obtained a special permit to bring a car inside the enclosure. Two jeeps were parked in the lee of the gatehouse, as usual, and they switched on their spotlights as Ambrose's car swept by, but neither of them followed. Snook wondered if the crews had been tipped off about Gene Helig's presence. In any case, he was glad Prudence had decided to remain at the hotel.

When he stepped out into the pre-dawn blackness he discovered he had become intensely aware of the stars. The constellations were glittering like cities in the sky, the colours of their individual stars easily distinguished, and Snook found himself grateful for their presence. He decided it was an unconscious reaction against his earlier vision of life on a blind planet, from which—even if the cloud cover were to vanish—it might not be possible to see the glowing stellar hearths of other civilisations. As he stood looking upwards, he vowed that when he got clear of Barandi he would take a positive interest in astronomy.

"There's nothing to see up there, old boy," Helig said jovially. "I'm told it's all below ground these days."

"That's right." Snook shivered in a river of cold air, shoved his hands deep into his jacket pockets and followed the rest of the group into descending cages. Ambrose had calculated that top dead centre for the Avernians would occur just above one of the worked-out pipes on Level Two. It was not an ideal location, because the Avernians would rise up into the rock ceiling for a few minutes, but the relative movement would be fairly slow and there would be two good opportunities for what Ambrose, in a resurgence of good spirits, had described as an "inter-universal *tête-à-tête*."

When he stepped on to the circular gallery of Level Two, Snook was relieved to find that his apprehension of the previous day had faded. The first instant of union with Felleth had been shocking, but not so much for its strangeness but its effectiveness. He had entered a mind, an intelligence which was the product of an unknown continuum, and yet it had been less alien to him than the minds of many human beings he had met. There had been in it, Snook believed, no capacity for murder or greed; and his certainty on this point made him marvel, yet again, that such a strange mode of communication should have been possible at all.

Ambrose had been emphatic in denying the possibility of previous long-range telepathic links between Avernians and humans—but, at the same time, Ambrose had confessed in the car that day that his knowledge of his specialist subject, nuclear physics, was faulty. He, Gilbert Snook, had suddenly become the world's foremost expert on mind-to-mind data transfer—admittedly without intending to do so—and it satisfied his sense of the fitness of things to postulate that Avernians and human beings, living on concentric biospheres for millions of years, had telepathically influenced each other's mental processes. The theory would account, perhaps, for the odd coincidence of words which Prudence had discovered, and for the widespread belief among primitive societies that another world existed below the surface of the Earth. Above all, and most important in Snook's opinion, it accounted for the compatibility of thought modes which made communication possible in the first place.

As he walked around the gallery to the pipe where the other men had gathered, Snook wondered if he could play the role of scientific researcher and take his theory one experimental step further. Having made the initial mental contact with Felleth—could he now, by conscious effort, reach him over a distance? The range would not be all that great, because at that moment Felleth would be somewhere below him and rising up through the rock strata, but the principle could be proved. He stopped walking, took off his Amplites, closed his eyes and tried to screen his brain from all sensory inputs. Feeling selfconscious, and aware that he was probably guilty of monstrous clumsiness in Avernian terms, he strove to form a mental picture of Felleth and to project the Avernian's name across the gulf which separated two universes.

In his mind there was nothing. Against the screen of his eyelids there was nothing, save the slow drifting of after-images conjured by his retinas. The random patterns of pseudo-light continued to merge and mingle, then—very gradually—Snook began to feel he could see something behind them. A pale green wall which was not a wall because it was possessed of movement, and endless rising and overturning and falling of its elements; there was translucency coupled with strength; a sense of solidity and liquidity; a changeless state of eternal changing . . .

Deep peace of the running . . .

"Come on, Gil," Ambrose called. "We're nearly all set up. Getting it down to a fine art."

Helig was standing beside Snook, the collar of his rollneck sweater pulled up over his chin. "Yes, come and join us—there's no show without Punch, is there?"

Snook blinked at the two men and fought to hide his annoyance. Had he been working a confidence trick on himself? Had the words begun to form in his mind because he had been expecting them? How could a telepath distinguish between his own thoughts and those of another?

"Snap out of it, old boy," Helig said, amiably impatient. "Have you been at the mother's ruin again?"

"What the hell's the rush?" Snook demanded. "We can't do anything until the Avernians get up to this level."

"Oh!" Helig raised his eyebrows. "Listen to our prima bloody donna!" He punched Snook playfully on the shoulder.

Snook fended off a second blow and forced himself to relax as they walked along the hollowed-out pipe to the area which Ambrose and Murphy, using drawings of the mine and a surveyor's tape, had marked off as the scene of operations. He was going to have his fill of telepathic experimentation in a matter of minutes, assuming that Felleth kept the implicit rendezvous. Ambrose, satisfied now that he had got his little team together, went on ahead to supervise Quig and Culver.

"Gene, you know this country better than most," Snook said in a quiet voice. "How long do you think Ogilvie will tolerate this mine being shut down?"

"Strangely enough, the President is taking it quite well. He's been flattered by the publicity Barandi has got out of it —these things are important to him—and I think he might be in two minds about what he ought to do. Tommy Freeborn is getting restless, though." Helig's face was unreadable behind the dark lenses of his Amplites. "Very restless."

"Think he's getting ready to answer the call of destiny?"

"I don't know what you mean."

"Come on, Gene—everybody knows Freeborn would like to give the two fingers to the United Nations, seal up the borders and get rid of all the whites and Asians."

"All right, but I didn't tell you this." Helig glanced around him, as if expecting to see microphones projecting from the stone. "The smart money has started to flow out of the country. I can't see Tommy Freeborn letting that go on for more than a week."

"I see. Are you leaving?"

Helig looked surprised. "Just when I'll have some real work to do?"

"Your Press card won't mean anything to the Colonel."

"It means something to me, old boy."

"I admire your principles," Snook said, "but I won't be around to see them put into practice."

They reached the other members of the group and Snook stood apart, trying to get his thoughts in order. The time had come for him to move on. All the signs were there, all the warnings had been sounded loud and clear, and although he had allowed himself to become involved in other people's problems, it was a mistake which could be rectified. It now seemed inevitable that there would be a Sharpesville-type slaughter of miners, but there was nothing he could do about that, and his worrying about it would have a negative result. Nature had yet to design a nervous system which was capable of sustaining the guilt of others.

Ambrose and Prudence represented a separate issue. They were sophisticated, well-educated adults—and the fact that he saw them as innocents abroad did not make him responsible for their welfare. Prudence Devonald, in particular, would resent it if he tried to offer advice, and if she wanted to hitch her wagon to Ambrose . . .

The trend of his thinking filled Snook with sudden self-doubt. Would he have been coolly planning to cut and run if Prudence had fallen into his arms after the incident in the Cullinan? The storybooks all agreed that was the appropriate reward for a knight who rescued a damsel in distress, but was it possible that he—Gilbert Snook, the human neutrino—had seriously expected her to translate romance to reality? And was it equally possible that he was preparing to abandon her in a fit of adolescent pique?

Disturbed at having blundered into emotional quicksands, Snook was almost relieved to see Ambrose studying his watch and giving the fluttering hand signals which indicated that top dead centre was imminent. Ambrose made some final adjustments to the boson field generator, and began explaining the entire procedure for Helig's benefit. There was less room than in the tunnels where the previous contacts had been made, and the members of the group were standing quite close together when the now-familiar glowing blue line appeared on the rock floor.

"Lateral displacement less than one metre," Ambrose murmured into his wrist recorder. Quig's camera began clicking in the background.

Snook moved forward, eager and reluctant at the same time, and stood perfectly still as the line rose upward to become the apex of a triangular prism of luminosity. The prism expanded upwards and outwards until its peak was above Snook's head and he could see the ghostly geometries of roof structure all about him. The horizontal plane of a ceiling came next, rising over his ankles and knees like the surface of an insubstantial lake. Snook knelt to bring his head down into the volume of the Avernian room. The three translucent figures were waiting for him, Felleth in the centre, growing upwards from the solid rock like sculpted columns of bluish smoke.

Felleth moved closer to Snook, on legs that were as yet invisible, and his arms were outstretched. Again the mist-pools of his eyes grew large. Snook inclined his head forward and, even before the contact was made, he could see the shimmering movement of the sea-green wall . . .

Deep peace of the running wave.

I ask your forgiveness, Equal Gil. I was at fault for not understanding that you are not accustomed to the congruency of self which you refer to as telepathy. A few unfortunate members of our race are afflicted with the silence that separates and, in my egotism, I presumed that you were similarly flawed because you issued no greeting. I was glad to feel you trying to make contact with me a short while ago, because it showed that you had come to no harm as a result of my mistake. During this meeting I am using purely sequential thought structures to avoid overloading your neural pathways. This technique, which we use in the teaching of our

*children, reduces the rate of information transfer, but there
will be a gain in effectiveness because your mind will be able
to function in an approximation of its normal manner.*

*I ask your forgiveness, too, because in my blind pride I
dared reject your stone house of proven knowledge in favour
of my reed hut of conjecture. My only excuse is that I was
shocked and in considerable pain—in one second I was given
more new knowledge than has been accumulated by the People in the last million days, and much of the knowledge was
of a kind I would have been happier not to have. I confess
that I was also confused and alarmed by the nature of your
arrival. The People have many myths about strange beings
who live in the clouds, and when you descended from the sky
it seemed to me—for an instant—that all the old superstitions
had been proved true. This, of course, is a feeble excuse for
my reaction, because the nature of your arrival was in itself a
proof of all your claims. A moment of logical consideration
would have shown that the vertical displacement of your
body relative to mine was generated by a hypocycloid of
planetary scale. Once that elementary step had been taken, all
the other deductions were inevitable, including the final one
concerning the fate of my world.*

Snook: I'm sorry that I was the bringer of such news.

*Do not distress yourself. The intellectual experience has
been unique—and the end is not yet. Also, the knowledge you
gave me has been put to good use. I have, for example, been
able to explain to the satisfaction of the People certain disturbing phenomena which have occurred in distant lands, all
of them near the equal-day line, which you refer to as the
equator. Some individuals have been terrified by visions, and
by intimations about the end of our world. Without knowing
it, for there was nothing to see, they had come within self-
congruency range of others of your race who live on or near
your equator, and an accidental and partial communication
was achieved.*

How is it that I am able to see you and your companions?

*Please be at ease—it is not necessary for you to construct
sentences, nor have we time for such laborious methods. You
have a companion who has knowledge of nuclear physics and*

it was his idea to illuminate your body by placing it within what he calls an intermediate vector boson field. I wish to communicate with him, but he is surrounded by the silence which separates and I have no means of reaching him. It is a pity that the planetary motion gives us such a short time together, but there is something you can do to help, if you are willing.

Snook: I'll do anything I can.

I am grateful. When we are separated from each other, please obtain writing materials and have them in your hands when we are united again. I will then be able to communicate with Equal Boyce. In addition, I have a very important request to make of you and all the other members of your race. I have learned that yours is a troubled and divided world, and in order that my request be properly received I must teach you enough about the People to make it clear that the granting of the request will not add to your problems. In a few seconds we will separate, therefore—to achieve my purpose—I must resort to full congruency of self. Do not be alarmed, and do not at this stage attempt to impose language upon concept.

Simply receive . . .

> *. . . the People are mammalian, bisexual, vegetarian (images of many Avernians, idealised/transformed by Felleth's own vision; underwater farms; swimmers tending lines of tree-like plants)*

> *. . . average life span is ninety-two of your/our years (unfamiliar method of reckoning)*

> *. . . inter-personal communication is telepathic, complemented by vocal sound, expression and gesture (images of Avernian faces, idealised/transformed, made meaningful, fierce white light of truth)*

> *. . . social organisation is paternal, flexible, informal— no equivalent term available in Earth languages (images of philosopher-statesmen holding congress in vast brown stone building covering two islands linked by a double-arched bridge)*

> *. . . mass aggression and individual aggression unknown in recent history—corrective procedure for murder*

*was voluntary cessation of breeding by all Aver-
nians of same genetic strain*
(*image of small wave losing momentum, subsiding
into the unity of the ocean*)
. . . *planetary population is now 12,000,000 but was
47,000,000 before the weight of the oceans decreased* (*images of bodies of small children floating
in water, faces downward, numerous as autumn
leaves on a forest floor, unmoving except for the
slow jostling of the waves*)

"Oh, God," Snook whispered. "It's too much. Too much."

He became aware of the pressure of the uneven rock
against his knees. His hands were holding the smooth plastic
frame of his magniluct glasses, and a flashlight beam was
dancing behind the silhouettes of human beings, shadows
flailing and flickering in the confines of the tunnel.

"Well I'll be damned," Helig said. "I never saw anything
like that."

Murphy and Helig came forward and helped Snook to his
feet. He looked around him and saw that Ambrose was close
by, still wearing his Amplites, busy chalking marks on the
tunnel wall, consulting his watch and talking into his recorder
in a low voice. Quig was operating his camera, pointing it upwards, and Culver was doubled over the rectangular shape of
the pulse code modulator. For an instant the scene was completely meaningless to Snook and he felt lost, then there was a
shift of perception, and the strangers became known to him,
their motivations familiar.

"How long did it last this time?" Snook's throat was dry,
hoarsening his voice. "How long was I in contact?"

"Your forehead was touching Felleth's for nearly a minute," Murphy said. "Was it Felleth, by the way?"

"Yes, that was Felleth."

"They all look alike to me," Murphy commented drily.
"Then he leaned forward and his head was right inside yours,
the way it was yesterday, for about a second."

"A second?" Snook pressed the back of a hand to his forehead. "I can't go on like this. I spend my whole life avoiding people, because I just don't want to know, and now . . ."

"They've gone," Ambrose said in a firm voice. "Everybody take their Amplites off—I'm turning on the big light." A moment later the tunnel was filled with marble-white brilliance. There was a general shuffling of feet and flexing of shoulders. Snook felt in his pocket for his cigarettes.

"We can relax for ten minutes until the Avernians pass top dead centre and drop down again," Ambrose continued.

"We drew a blank on the modulator," Culver said. "I don't think they were trying for light-sound communication this time—at least, I didn't see any equipment."

"No, it looks as though they've decided to work through Gil." Ambrose lit Snook's cigarette and his voice became unexpectedly sympathetic. "How was it, Gil? Rough?"

Snook inhaled fragrant smoke. "If anybody ever shoves an air hose in your ear and inflates your head to five times its normal size, you'll get some idea."

"Can you give me a preliminary report?"

"Not now—I'll need a full morning with a recorder." There was an abrupt stirring in Snook's memory. "Felleth is going to send you a message, Boyce. I need a writing block and a pen before he comes back again."

"A message? Have you any idea what it could be?"

"It's technical. And it's something big . . ." Snook felt the coldness of prescience beginning to grow within him and he fought to quell it. "Just give me the block and pen, will you?"

"Of course."

Snook took the writing equipment, moved a short distance down the tunnel from the rest of the group and stood by himself. He lit a second cigarette and smoked it with quiet concentration, all the while wishing he was far away and above ground, in sunlight. The sunlight was important. There had to be clear skies, with views of infinity, a visual antidote to the blind grey skies of Avernus. There had to be an escape from the claustrophobic, doomed world, with its low islands reflecting as diamond-shapes in the tideless ocean, and the bodies of alien children drifting like sterile spawn . . .

"Ready for you, Gil," Ambrose called, and at the same moment the tunnel was returned to its former state of darkness. Snook put on his Amplites, creating a spurious blue radiance in which his cigarette end shone with magnified brilliance. He ground it out under his heel and walked back to the arena.

Deep peace of the running wave.

You will be interested to learn, Equal Gil, that although the People's transportation systems have largely been destroyed, our communications were not affected by the disaster a thousand days ago. The possibility of using electrical phenomena to transmit signals over great distances has been known to us for a long time—and we have demonstrated the method for purely scientific reasons—but for all general communications we rely on the congruency of self, which you know as telepathy.

In this way, the knowledge you brought me yesterday has already been disseminated to all of the People. The Responders have held communion and given their advice, and a decision has been made. It is contrary to our philosophy to surrender life to the forces of entropy, but we have agreed that we do not want our children's children to be born into a world which can offer them nothing but death. Accordingly, we will cease to fertilise our females.

It is not difficult for us—a logical consequence of our form of telepathy is voluntary control over the proto-minds of our seedlings. This has given us predetermination of the sex of our offspring, and it also permits us to choose sterility if we so desire.

We have been fortunate—some would say a greater power has ordained it—in that the time remaining to our world is slightly greater than the average lifetime of our individual members. A small proportion of the People will therefore continue to produce children for another four hundred days. It will be the melancholy duty of this final generation to act as caretakers for the rest of us, to oversee our departure from life, and to organise our dwindling resources in such a way that in the last days there will be no starvation, no depriva-

tion, no suffering, no loss of dignity. When the oceans rise again they will bring neither fear nor death—for we shall have gone.

Snook: How can you make a unanimous decision like that in such a short time?

The People are not like human beings. I am not claiming that we are superior—it can be expected of any telepathic society that reason, which reinforces itself and grows stronger on the universality of truth, will prevail over unreason, which grows less coherent and weaker as its individual proponents are isolated in their own unrealities. The People will act in concert, as one, in this final trial, as in the lesser ordeals of the past.

Snook: But how can they accept it so quickly when only two days ago you had no science of astronomy? How do they know that what I told you was true?

I do not know if you will be able to understand the difference in our philosophies, but the only reason we did not have a science of astronomy is that we had no requirement for it. It would have served no purpose. Our physics are not your physics. I have learned, from your store of knowledge, that you have a science of radio astronomy, with instruments which would tell you of the existence of other worlds and other stars even if Earth was permanently covered by cloud— but, although wave phenomena are similar in my universe, such instruments have not been constructed here because we could not have conceived a use for them. However, when we were presented with the evidence of your experience we were quite capable of using it as a foundation and building an appropriate logical edifice. The People were not persuaded by you, or by me. They were persuaded by truth.

Snook: But so quickly!

It is not the speed of acceptance which perplexes you, but the acceptance itself. But do not be deceived into thinking there is no grief. We are neither passive nor submissive. The People are not content to bow out of existence. We accept that the vast majority of our race must cease to exist, but as long as a few of us survive our life-wave will be preserved and may grow strong again some day.

Snook: Is that possible? I've been told that your world will be totally destroyed—so how will it be possible for any of you to survive?

There is only one way in which we can survive, Equal Gil —and that is by entering your world.

On behalf of the People . . . and in the name of Life . . . I am asking your race to make room for us on Earth.

The bright light had been switched on again, transforming the tunnel into a pantomime setting, and the cast of strangers was assembled as before. Snook stared at each in turn, until they had assumed their identities. Murphy was looking at him with a slight frown, but the other men were standing near the light and their attention was focused on a flat rectangular object. It took Snook a few seconds to identify it as the writing pad which Ambrose had given him. Ambrose raised his eyes in a long, level stare.

"What is this, Gil?" he said. "What's happening here?"

Snook flexed his fingers, trying to orient himself in his own body. "I'm sorry. Felleth must have forgotten to give me the message, or perhaps there wasn't enough time."

"I've *got* the message! Look at it!" Ambrose held the pad in front of Snook's face. The entire top sheet was covered with words and mathematical symbols, laid out in perfectly straight lines as if they had been typed.

Snook touched the block with his fingertips, feeling the faint indentations caused by the pen. "Did I do that?"

"In about thirty seconds flat, old boy," Helig said. "I tell you, I've never seen anything like it. I've heard of automatic writing, but I never really believed in it till now. I tell you, this is . . ."

"We can go into that later," Ambrose cut in. "Gil, do you know what this is?"

Snook swallowed with difficulty, playing for time in which to think. "What does it look like to you?"

"These equations appear to outline a process, using inverse beta-decay, which would transmute anti-neutrino matter into protons and neutrons," Ambrose said in a sombre voice. "At first glance it looks like a proposal for transferring objects from the Avernian universe into this one."

"You've almost got it right," Snook replied, reassured at hearing what might have been his own private fantasy voiced by another human being. "But Felleth wasn't talking about transferring objects—he wants to send us some of his people."

CHAPTER ELEVEN

They returned to the car in silence, each man in the lonely fortress of his own thoughts, and loaded it with the various items of equipment. On reaching the surface, Snook had not been surprised to note that the sky had clouded over in preparation for the grass rains which would last for approximately two weeks. It was as though the world was trying to model itself on his vision of Avernus, making ready for visitors. He shivered and rubbed his hands together, discovering as he did so that his right hand and forearm were curiously numb and tired. The group got into the car, with Ambrose taking the wheel, and the heavy silence continued until the vehicle had passed out through the gates of the mine enclosure.

"Gil's phone is out of action," Ambrose said, turning to Helig. "I suppose the first thing we should do is get you to another one."

Helig smiled complacently and his eyelids drooped more than was usual. "It isn't necessary, old boy. I'm accustomed to telephones mysteriously breaking down everywhere I go these days—so I brought a radio transmitter." He tapped his jacket pocket. "I'll file my story through a colleague in Matsa. All I need is somewhere to sit in peace for twenty minutes."

"That's easily arranged. Are you going to write out your story for me to vet it?"

"Sorry—I don't work that way."

"I thought you might want me to check the science."

"I've done all the double-checking that's necessary." Helig gave Ambrose a quizzical glance. "Besides, the science isn't important—this is a news story."

Ambrose shrugged and switched on the windscreen wipers as the first drops of rain began to shatter themselves on the dusty glass in front of him. The dust was momentarily smeared into two brownish sectors which disappeared as the rain grew heavier. There was another silence which lasted until they had stopped at the bungalow, at which point Ambrose turned right round in his seat and tapped Quig's knee. Quig, who had been sitting with nodding head and closed eyes, gave a start.

"Didn't you say you have a friend in the lab at the new power station?" Ambrose said.

"Yes. Jack Postlethwaite. He came out at the same time as Benny and myself."

"Do you know for certain that they have a Moncaster machine in the laboratory?"

"I think so. Isn't it something like a signal generator, except that it gives you different kinds of radiation fields?"

"That's exactly what it is." Ambrose took the ignition keys from the dash and dropped them into Quig's hand. "Des, I want you and Benny to take my car, drive over to the power station right now and hire that machine from your friend."

Quig's jaw sagged. "But those things cost a fortune—and this isn't even Jack's property."

Ambrose opened his wallet, took out a thousand-dollar bill and dropped it in Quig's lap. "That's for your friend, for a couple of days' hire of the machine. There'll be the same amount for you when you get back, to divide between you—provided you have the machine with you? Okay?"

"You bet it's okay." While Culver nodded vigorously, Quig scrambled out of the car, sped round it to the driver's door and stood jigging in the rain while Ambrose got out.

"Not so fast," Ambrose said to him. "We still have to unship our gear."

Snook, who had been watching the transaction with interest, kept an eye on Ambrose during the unloading operation. Overnight the scientist seemed to have grown a little older, a little harder around the eyes and mouth, and he was moving with the jerky energy of a man whose mind was on fire. As soon as the car had swished away down the hill with Quig at the wheel, Ambrose gave Snook a wry grin.

"Let's go inside," he said. "You've got one hell of a debriefing session in front of you."

Snook remained leaning against a wooden upright of the verandah. "Let's stay out here for a minute."

"Why?"

"Because it's more private than in the house. You know, of course, that young Quig and Culver and their friend could get jail—or worse—if they're caught borrowing that machine. The power station is state property."

"They won't get caught," Ambrose said easily. He opened a pack of cigarettes and handed one to Snook.

"Do you need that machine to bring the Avernians through to Earth?"

"Yes. They couldn't do it if we didn't help by setting up the right local environment. I'll have to get a supply of hydrogen today, as well."

"What's all the hurry?" Snook stared hard at Ambrose's face above the transparent blue shoot of his lighter flame. "Why do you have to try this thing when the conditions are all wrong?"

"I disagree with you about the conditions, Gil—they'll never be as good again. You know that tomorrow top dead centre will occur just a couple of metres above ground level, but from then on Avernus will permanently be swelling out through the Earth's surface. It'll be like a flat dome which gets five hundred metres higher every day. That may not seem like much, but we're dealing with a tangent which is practically zero, which means that the edge of that dome will be spreading out in all directions at tremendous speed.

"True there'll be two lesser top dead centres, one north of the equator and one south of it, but they'll be running away from the equator all the time, and it will be difficult to set up equipment at one of them and hold station with respect to a corresponding point on Avernus. This time, right now, is the only time when we'll only have to deal with movement in one sense . . ." Ambrose halted the flow of words, meeting Snook's gaze.

"But those weren't the conditions you meant, were they?"

"No."

"You were asking why I want to try it when we're stuck in the middle of nowhere, surrounded by trigger-happy stormtroopers who would shoot us as soon as look at us."

"Something like that," Snook said.

"Well, one reason is that nobody in the world today is going to like the idea of a race of alien supermen muscling in on what's left of our resources. The UN is likely to veto the whole thing on quarantine reasons alone, so it would be better to aim for a *fait accompli*. The chance is too good to miss." Ambrose put his finger into a domed raindrop on the verandah railing and smeared it out flat.

"What's the other reason?"

"I got on to this thing first. I came here first. It's mine, Gil, and I *need* it. This is my one chance to be the person I set out to be a long time ago—can you understand that?"

"I think so, but does it mean so much that you don't care about people getting hurt?"

"I don't want anybody to get hurt—besides, I don't think I could drive Des and Benny off with a shotgun."

"I was thinking more about Prudence," Snook said. "Why don't you use your influence with her and get her out of the country?"

"She's her own woman, Gil." Ambrose sounded unconcerned as he turned to go indoors. "What makes you think I've got any influence in that direction?"

"You've slept with her, haven't you?" Snook was unable to keep the bitterness out of his voice. "Or doesn't that count any more?"

"That's *all* I've done—slept with her. I was too whacked for anything else that morning." Ambrose looked at Snook with new interest. "It's a good thing I was pole-axed—it probably spared me an embarrassing scene."

"How?"

"Our Miss Devonald isn't as casual about sex as she likes people to believe. It's when you try to treat her like a woman that she begins acting like a man. And not just any man. General George S. Patton, I'd say." Ambrose walked to the door of the house and then came back.

"How about you, Gil?" he said. "Are you going to pull out on me?"

"No. I'll stay around."

"Thanks—but why?"

Snook gave him a brief smile. "Would you believe it's because I like Felleth?"

By the last decade of the twentieth century the standard of living in even the most advanced of the world's countries had become patchy. The Orwellian prediction that people would be able to afford nothing but luxuries had been amply fulfilled. It was, for example, difficult to obtain a safely edible fish, and the World Health Organisation had solemnly, and with every appearance of conviction, halved its mid-century estimate of the number of grammes of first-class protein that an adult needed each day to maintain good health.

On the other hand, communications were excellent—the synchronous satellite and the germanium diode ensured that practically everybody on the planet could be informed of an important event within minutes of its occurrence. It was, however, only possible to broadcast information—not understanding—and there were many who maintained that people in general would have been better off, certainly happier, without the ceaseless welter of news which bombarded them from the skies. The principal achievement of the telecommunications industry, they claimed, was that it was now possible to start in minutes the same riot that would have required days a few decades earlier.

Gene Helig's account of the events in Barandi National Mine No. 3 was in the hands of his colleague in the neighbouring statelet of Matsa before 8.00 a.m. local time, and in a further ten minutes had been relayed to the Press Association office in Salisbury, Rhodesia. Because both journalists concerned had the highest professional credentials, the story was accepted without question and beamed via satellite to several

major centres, including London and New York. From there
it was shared out among other agencies with special ethnic,
cultural, political or geographical interests. Up to that point
the original message had been analogous to the output grid
current in a thermionic valve, a puny trickle of electrons, but
its characteristics were suddenly amplified by the full power
of the global news services and it began to surge massively
from pole to pole, swamping the various media. Again as in
the case of a thermionic valve, excessive amplification led in-
evitably to distortion.

The reactions were almost immediate.

Tensions had been high in those equatorial countries in
which the Avernians had been sighted, and the news that the
immaterial "ghosts" were planning to turn themselves into
solid, substantial, material invaders caused people to take to
the streets. The terminator, the line which divided night from
day—and which also marked the emergence point of the alien
planet and its inhabitants—was proceeding westwards along
the equator at a leisurely rate of less then 1,700 kilometres an
hour, and thus was far outstripped by the rumours of the
menace it was supposed to represent. While morning sunlight
was filtering down through the rain clouds which covered
Barandi, the darkness which still lay over Ecuador, Columbia
and three of the new countries which occupied northern Brazil was disturbed here and there by the classical symptoms of
panic. And far to the north, in New York, members of several special United Nations committees were summoned from
their beds.

President Paul Ogilvie read carefully through the news
summary sheets and memoranda which had been left for his
attention by his personal secretary, then he pressed a switch
on his communicator set and said, "I want Colonel Freeborn
here immediately."

He took a cigar from the silver box on his desk and busied
himself with the rituals of removing the band, cutting the
sealed end and ensuring that the tobacco was ignited evenly.
His hands remained perfectly steady throughout the entire

operation, but he was not concealing from himself the fact that he had been shocked by the news he had just read. His other self, the one which obstinately clung to the old tribal name with which he had begun life, felt a deep unease at the idea of ghosts stalking among the lakeside trees, and the prospect of the ghosts materialising into solid flesh smacked even more clearly of magic. The fact that the paraphernalia of nuclear physics was involved did not prevent the magic from being magic—the knowledge that witch doctors used psychological techniques did nothing to render them harmless.

At another level of consciousness, Ogilvie was disturbed by a conviction that his present security and all his plans for the future were being threatened by the new developments at the mine. He enjoyed having fifty expensive suits and a fleet of prestige cars; he relished the superb food and wine, and the exotic women which he imported like any other luxury commodity; and, above all, he savoured Barandi's growing acceptance among the other countries of the world, the imminence of its full membership of the United Nations. Barandi was his own personal creation, and official recognition by the UN would be history's seal of approval upon Paul Ogilvie, the man.

He had more to lose than any other man in the country, and his instincts were keener in proportion—it was becoming obvious to him that the affair at Three had been mishandled. Swift, stern measures at the outset might have quashed the whole thing, but it was too late for that now, and the danger was that Freeborn might go off the rails in full view of the world. Now that he thought of it, Colonel Freeborn was fast becoming an anachronism and a liability in a number of respects . . .

The communicator set buzzed softly and his secretary announced the Colonel's arrival. "Send him in," Ogilvie said, closing a mental file for the time being.

"Afternoon, Paul." Freeborn strode into the big office with an air of barely controlled anger, his long-muscled galley slave's arms glistening beneath the half-sleeves of his drill shirt.

"Have you seen this stuff?" Ogilvie tapped the sheets on his blotter.

"I got my copies."

"What do you think?"

"I think we've been pussy-footing around for far too long, and this is the outcome. It's time we went in there . . ."

"I mean what do you think about these creatures from another world which are supposed to come through a machine?"

Freeborn looked surprised. "I don't think anything of it—partly because I don't believe in fairy tales, but mainly because I'm going to kick those white *wabwa* out of the mine before they cost us any more time and money."

"We can't do anything too hastily," Ogilvie said, examining the ash of his cigar. "I've just had word from New York that the United Nations is sending a team of investigators."

"United Nations! United Nations! That's all I hear from you these days, Paul." Freeborn clenched his fist around his gold-topped cane. "What has happened to you? This is *our* country—we don't have to let anybody in if we don't want them."

Ogilvie sighed, sending a flat cloud of grey smoke billowing on the polished wood of his desk. "Everything can be handled diplomatically. The UN people want Doctor Ambrose to stop whatever it is he's doing, which suits us perfectly. As a matter of interest, did your friend Snook make any attempt to contact you and keep you informed as we arranged?"

"I've had no messages from him."

"There you are! He ignored his brief, and that entitles me to tell him and Doctor Ambrose to get out of the mine. And we'll be complying with the UN's wishes."

Freeborn dropped into a chair and rested his forehead on one hand. "I swear to you, Paul—this is making me ill. I don't care about Ambrose, but I've got to have this man, Snook. If I sent the Leopards back into . . ."

"Are you sure they could deal with him, Tommy? I've heard that when he's armed with a piece of cutlery he can overcome a platoon of Leopards."

"I've just heard about that and haven't had time to investigate, but apparently there was an incident, a trivial incident, involving three of my men."

"Three men and an officer, wasn't it?"

Freeborn did not raise his head, but a vein began to pulse on his shaven temple. "What do you want me to do?"

"Get Snook's telephone line connected again," Ogilvie said. "I want to talk to him right now." He sat back in his chair and watched as Freeborn took a small military communicator from his shirt pocket and spoke into it, noting with amusement that—even for such a minor detail—the Colonel used a pre-arranged code word. A minute later Freeborn nodded and put his radio away. Ogilvie instructed his secretary to get Snook on the line. He stared thoughtfully at the rain-streaming windows, deliberately presenting the appearance of a man in effortless control of his circumstances, until the connection was made.

"Good afternoon, Snook," he said. "Is Doctor Ambrose with you?"

"No, sir. He's down at the mine setting up some equipment."

Freeborn stirred restlessly as Snook's voice reached him through the phone's loudspeaker attachment.

"In that case," Ogilvie said, "I'll have to deal with you, won't I?"

"Is there anything wrong, sir?" Snook sounded helpful, ready to please.

Ogilvie gave an appreciative laugh, recognising Snook's way of touching gloves with him. "There appear to be quite a few things wrong. I don't like having to listen to the British Broadcasting Corporation to find out what's happening in my country. What happened to our arrangement that you would keep Colonel Freeborn informed of all developments at the mine?"

"I'm sorry, sir—but things have been happening so quickly, and my telephone has been out of order. In fact, yours is the first call to get through for days. I don't understand how it happened, because I've never had any trouble with the tele-

phone before now. It might be something to do with the
. . ."

"Snook! Don't overdo it. What's all this about a plan to
make our so-called ghosts materialise into flesh and blood?"

"Is that what they said on the radio?"

"You know it is."

"Well, that's Doctor Ambrose's department, sir. I don't
even see how such a thing would be possible."

"Neither do I," Ogilvie said, "but apparently some of the
UN's science advisers think there could be something in it,
and they don't like the idea any more than I do. They're
sending a team of investigators with whom I'm going to co-
operate to the fullest extent. In the meantime, Doctor Ambrose is to suspend all activities. Is that clear?"

"Very clear, sir. I'll contact Doctor Ambrose at once."

"Do that." Ogilvie replaced the phone and sat tapping it
with a fingernail. "Your friend Snook is as slippery as an eel—
how many times did he address me as sir?"

Freeborn stood up, swinging his cane. "I'd better get out to
the mine and make sure they clear out of it."

"No. I want the Leopards pulled right out and I want you
to stay in Kisumu, Tommy—Snook gets under your skin too
easily. I don't want any more trouble than I've already got."
Ogilvie gave Freeborn a moody, speculative stare.

"Besides, we both agree that the whole thing about visitors
from another world is a ridiculous fairy tale."

CHAPTER TWELVE

Snook had just set off down the hill to the mine when an unfamiliar car pulled up beside him, its wheel arches cascading
yellowish muddy water. The passenger door opened and he
saw Prudence leaning across the seat towards him.

"Where's Boyce?" she said. "I don't see his car."

"He's at the mine setting up some new equipment. I'm on
my way to see him now."

"Jump in and I'll take you—it's too wet for walking." Prudence hesitated after Snook had got in. "Will it be safe for me to go to the mine?"

"It's all right—my friends drove off in their jeeps about an hour ago."

"They weren't your friends, Gil. I shouldn't have said anything like that."

"I shouldn't have raked it up again. It's just . . ." Snook held back the words which would make him vulnerable.

"Just what?" Prudence's eyes were steady on his own. She was still turned towards him, her skirt and blouse drawn tightly across her body in diagonal folds. Within the car, the dim afternoon light was reduced to a scented gloaming, the rain-fogged windows were screening off the rest of the world, and Prudence was smiling one of her rueful, perfect smiles.

"It's just," Snook said, his heart assuming a slow, powerful rhythm, "that I keep thinking about you all the time."

"Dreaming up fresh insults?"

Snook shook his head. "I'm jealous of you, and it's something that never happened to me before. When I walked into the Commodore, and saw you sitting with Boyce, I felt this pang of jealousy. It doesn't make any kind of sense, and yet I felt as if he'd robbed me. Since then . . ." Snook stopped speaking, finding it genuinely difficult to form words.

"What is it, Gil?"

"Do you know what's happening now?" He smiled at her. "I'm trying to make love to you without touching you—and it isn't easy."

Prudence touched his hand and he saw in her face the beginnings of a special, unique softness. Her lips parted slowly, almost reluctantly, and he was leaning forward to claim fulfilment when a rear door of the car was thrown open and George Murphy exploded into their presence in a fluster of plastic clothing, rain splashes and mint-smelling breath. The car rocked on its suspension with the impact of his body.

"That was a bit of luck," Murphy said breathlessly. "I thought I'd have to walk all the way to the mine in that stuff. What a bloody day!"

"Hi, George." Snook was oppressed by a sense of loss, of doors into the future closing with ponderous finality.

"You're going to the mine, aren't you?"

"Where else?" Prudence started the car moving down the hill and, in an immediate change of mood which filled Snook with an obscure pain, said, "Gil wants to try out a new plastic pick axe."

"It's bound to be better than the old-fashioned wood and steel jobs," Murphy chuckled. "Unless . . . Unless . . . How would it be if we tried making the *handles* out of wood and the blades out of steel?"

"Too revolutionary." Prudence flashed him a smile over her shoulder. "Everybody knows pick axes have to have wooden blades."

Unable to match the levity, Snook said, "I've just had a call from Ogilvie—he has ordered us out of the mine."

"Why's that?"

"I suppose it's a reasonable demand, from his point of view." Snook got a grim pleasure from stating the opposition case. "Boyce was sent into the mine to lay ghosts, not to materialise them."

They found Ambrose and Quig three hundred metres south of the mine head, working in a nondescript patch of flat ground which was used for the disposal of packing cases, scrap lumber and broken machine parts. Ambrose had calculated that the Avernians would attain an elevation of some two metres above ground at maximum, and he had constructed a makeshift platform of that height on which to place his equipment. He and Quig were soaked through, but were trudging about with a kind of water-logged cheerfulness which made Snook think of Great War soldiers giving thumbs-up signs for the benefit of correspondents' cameras. Already in place on the platform, and covered by a plastic sheet, was a bulky cube which Snook took to be the Moncaster machine. Ambrose came forward to meet the car, smiling uncertainly when he saw Prudence.

"What are you doing here?" he said, opening the driver's door.

Prudence took a handkerchief from her sleeve and dabbed

the rain from his face. "I've got a sense of history, *mon ami*. I've no intention of missing this show—provided there is a show, that is."

Ambrose frowned. "What does that mean?"

While Murphy got out of the car and distributed an armful of blue plastic raincoats, Snook gave Ambrose details of the telephone call from President Ogilvie. Ambrose accepted a raincoat, but made no move to put it on, and his mouth withered into a thin, hard line as he listened to Snook's report. He had begun shaking his head—slowly and steadily as an automaton—long before Snook had finished speaking.

"I'm not stopping," he said in a harsh, unrecognisable voice. "Not for President Paul Ogilvie. Not for anybody."

Lieutenant Curt Freeborn listened to the words with a deep satisfaction which went a long way towards soothing the anguish which had been burning inside him for many hours.

He removed the headphones of the telebug system, being careful to avoid disturbing the patch of gauze over his right eye, and put them in the carrying case alongside the associated sighting scope. The foreigners were hundreds of paces away from him and completely wrapped up in their own affairs, but nevertheless he crawled on his hands and knees for quite a long distance to obviate any risk of being seen as he was leaving his observation post. When he had cleared the angular jungle of the dumping area, he got to his feet, brushed the clinging mud and grass from his slickers, and walked quickly to the entrance gate. None of the mine guards in the security building would have dared question his movements, but he waved to them in a friendly manner as he left the enclosure. He had evidence which would justify firm action against Snook and the others, and his spirits had improved at the prospect. More important, he had evidence of his own resourcefulness and value as an officer in the Leopard Regiment, evidence his uncle would have to accept.

Crossing the puddled surface of the street, he sheltered in a doorway and took his communicator from an inner pocket.

There was a delay of only a few seconds while the local relay operator patched him through to his uncle's office in Kisumu.

"This is Curt," he said tersely on hearing his uncle's identification. "Are you free to speak?"

"I'm free to speak to you, Lieutenant, but I have no inclination to do so." Colonel Freeborn replied with the voice of a stranger, and the fact that he was using the formal mode of address was a bad omen.

"I've just carried out a solo reconnoitre at the mine," Curt said hurriedly. "I got close enough to hear what Snook and the *daktari* were saying, and . . ."

"How did you accomplish that?"

"Ah . . . I used one of the K.80 remote listening sets."

"I see—and did you bring it back with you?"

"Of course," Curt said indignantly. "Why do you ask?"

"I merely wondered if Mister Snook or his friend Murphy had decided to relieve you of it. From what I hear, you've been setting them up in the ex-army supplies business."

Curt felt a needle spray of ice on his forehead. "You've heard about . . ."

"I think everybody in Barandi has heard—including the President."

The sensation of stinging coldness began to spread over Curt's entire body, making him tremble. "It wasn't my fault. My men were . . ."

"Don't whine, Lieutenant. You went after a piece of white meat—regardless of my views on that sort of behaviour—and you let a couple of civilians disarm you in a public place."

"I recovered the Uzis a few minutes later." Curt did not mention that his automatic had not been found in the jeep.

"We can discuss the brilliance of your rearguard action at another time, when you're explaining why you didn't report the incident to me," Colonel Freeborn snapped. "Now get off the air and stop wasting my time."

"Wait," Curt said desperately, "you haven't heard my report about the mine."

"What about it?"

"They aren't leaving. They're planning to work on."

"So?"

"But the President wants them to leave." Curt was baffled by his uncle's reaction to his news. "Wasn't it a firm order?"

"Firm orders have gone out of fashion in Barandi," the Colonel said.

"With you, perhaps." Curt could feel himself nearing a precipice, but he plunged onwards. "But some of us haven't gone soft from sitting behind a desk all day."

"You are hereby suspended from duty," his uncle said in a cold, distant voice.

"You can't do this to me."

"I'd have done it sooner if I'd known where you were hiding. I've already awarded floggings to the three soldiers you contaminated with your ineptness and reduced them to kitchen patrol. In your case, though, I think a court martial is called for."

"No, uncle, no!"

"Do not address me in that manner."

"But I can get them out of the mine for you," Curt said, struggling against the wheedling note which was creeping into his voice. "The President will be pleased, and that'll make everything . . ."

"Wipe your nose, Lieutenant," the Colonel ordered. "And when you have finished wiping it, report to barracks. That is all."

Curt Freeborn stared incredulously at his communicator for a moment, then he opened his fingers and let it fall to the concrete at his feet. Its pea-sized function indicator light continued to glow like a cigarette end in the gathering dimness. He smashed a metal-shod heel down on it, then stepped out into the rain, his smooth young face as impenetrable as that of an ebony carving.

At nightfall Ambrose called a temporary halt to the work and the group moved under the platform to drink coffee which he shared out from a huge flask. The rain had begun to ease off slightly and the presence of refreshments, coupled with the jostling comradeship, made the crude shelter seem cosy. They had been joined by Gene Helig, who added to the picnic atmosphere by producing a paper bag full of chocolate bars and a bottle of South African brandy. Culver and Quig became cheerfully intoxicated almost at once.

Twice during the amiable scrimmage Snook found himself standing next to Prudence. Selfconsciously, like a schoolboy, he attempted to touch her hand—hoping to recreate something of the former moment of intimacy—but each time she moved away, seemingly oblivious to his presence, leaving him feeling thwarted and lonely.

Automatically, he countered with the defence measures which had served him without fail for many years in many countries. He threw the coffee from his cup, filled it to the brim with brandy, retreated to the outer edge of the shelter and lit a cigarette. The neat spirit kindled a fire inside him, but it was fighting a losing battle with the darkness which pressed in from the wilderness outside. Snook began to develop a gloomy conviction that Ambrose's enterprise was about to go disastrously wrong. He glanced around without interest as Ambrose came to stand beside him.

"Don't weaken," Ambrose said. "We'll be pulling out in the morning."

"You're sure about that?"

"Positive. I had planned to follow later top dead centres up into the sky, but it's all becoming too difficult—I cancelled the helicopter today. I doubt if I would have been allowed to use it anyway."

Snook swallowed more brandy. "Boyce, what makes you so positive that Felleth will be ready to attempt a transfer next time around?"

"He's a scientist. He knows as well as I do that tomorrow morning we'll have optimum conditions for the experiment."

"Optimum, but not unique. I've been thinking about what you said, and I can see that when the surface of Avernus comes out through the Earth there'll be two top dead centres, one heading north and one heading south, but that only applies to this longitude, doesn't it? And what if they *are* moving? With a bit of time in hand, and international funding, you could beat that problem. And what about the poles? There must be very little movement there—just the sideslip."

"You have been thinking, haven't you?" Ambrose raised his cup in mock toast. "Where would the international funding come from? It's the UN that's trying to block us right now."

"But that's only their first reaction."

"You want to bet?"

"All right—but what about the other points?"

"Can the Avernians travel round their equator at will? Have they got land in their temperate zones? Can they even reach their north and south poles?"

Snook delved into his fragmentary second memory. "I don't think so, but . . ."

"Believe me, Gil, tomorrow morning is the right time for this experiment."

Snook was raising his cup to his lips when the significance of Ambrose's final word reached him. "Wait a minute—that's the second time you've called it an experiment. Do you mean it isn't all cut and dried?"

"Hardly." Ambrose gave Snook a strangely wan smile. "That piece of paper you wrote on will advance our nuclear science by twenty years when I get it back to the States, but your friend Felleth is pushing his theoretical physics to the limit. I've looked at his equations and interactions, but—quite frankly—I'm not good enough to predict whether they'll work or not. They seem all right to me, but I'm not sure if Felleth will get through. There's also the possibility that he could make it and be dead on arrival."

Snook was appalled by the new information. "And you're still going to try it?"

"I thought you would understand, Gil," Ambrose said. "Felleth has to take this one ideal chance to prove that transfers are possible. His people need a ray of hope, and they need it fast. That's why we're committed."

"Then . . . you think that if you get proof the system works Earth will let them in later on?"

Ambrose grinned handsomely, tilting his cigarette with his lips like a matinée idol. "Learn to think big, Gil. Times change—and there's almost a century to play with. Fifty years from now we might be ferrying Avernians down out of the sky in spaceships."

"Well, I'll be . . ." Snook was impelled to grip the other man's hand. "You know, I had you down as a self-centred bastard."

"I am," Ambrose assured him. "It's just pure luck that this time I get a chance to disguise the fact."

At that moment they were joined by George Murphy, who was nursing his bandaged right hand. "I'm going over to the medical building to get myself a shot of something for this hand. I think I've toted too many bales with it, whatever that means."

"I'll drive you there," Ambrose said.

"No. I can do it on foot in a couple of minutes, and the rain has almost stopped." Murphy set off into the blackness.

"I'll go with you," Snook called after him, running to catch up. When they passed out of range of Ambrose's portable lights the going became treacherous and both men had to walk carefully, even with their Amplites on, until they reached the misty green radiance which surrounded the mine buildings. The medical building was as dark and lifeless as all the others in the vicinity.

"Here's the keys." Murphy handed Snook a jingling cluster. "Can you pick out number eight for me?"

"I expect so. If I can rebuild an aero engine I ought to be able . . ." Snook held still for a second, his senses probing the shadowed environment, then he lowered his voice. "Don't look round, George—there's somebody behind you."

"That's funny," Murphy whispered, his left hand fumbling with the fastenings of his raincoat. "I was going to say the same thing to you."

"*Don't move!*" The command came from a tall young man who had stepped into view from around a corner of the low building. He was wearing army slickers and a helmet with a lieutenant's bars on it, and there was a patch of white gauze over his right eye. A deep sadness welled up in Snook as he recognised Curt Freeborn. He glanced around him, assessing the chances of getting away, and saw three soldiers with drawn bush knives hemming them in. They were the same men he had encountered at the Cullinan, and they gave the impression of being determined that things would work out differently this time.

"What a stroke of luck!" Freeborn said. "My two favourite people—the funny white man, and his Uncle Tom."

Snook and Murphy looked at each other without speaking.

"No funny remarks, Mister Snook?" Freeborn began to smile. "Aren't you feeling well?"

"What I'd like to know," Murphy said, his left hand still working with the stiff, slippery plastic fastenings of his coat, "is why four so-called Leopards are crawling around in the dark like rats."

"I wasn't speaking to you, trash."

"Take it easy, George," Snook said anxiously.

"But this is an interesting point," Murphy pressed on. "The Colonel, for instance, would have come in with lights blazing. It seems to me that . . ."

Freeborn gave a slight nod of his head, and almost immediately something struck Murphy in the back. The blow was so noisy, accompanied by a flapping crack of plastic, that Snook thought the corporal had slapped the big man with the flat of his bush knife. Then he saw Murphy going down on his knees and, from a corner of his eye, the corporal pulling the blade back with difficulty. He caught hold of Murphy and felt the dreadful looseness of muscle and limb, a dead weight which pulled him inexorably downwards. Snook knelt, cradling Murphy in his left arm, and ripped open his coat. He slid his hand inside, feeling for a heartbeat, and was horrified to discover—even though the thrust had been at the back—that the whole chest region was bathed in a hot wetness. Murphy's mouth sagged open and, even in death, he smelled of mint.

"That was too quick," Freeborn said to the corporal, his voice mildly reproachful, face impassive behind his Amplites. "You let the Uncle Tom out too soon."

"You . . ." Snook tried to speak, but his throat closed on the words, the words which in any case would have failed to express his grief and hatred. He hugged Murphy's body to him and his right hand, sliding in blood, encountered a hard-

edged, familiar shape. At that moment it was the most beautiful shape in the world, with a metallic perfection far beyond
that of a priceless sculpture. Keeping his head lowered, Snook
looked around him. He could see four pairs of legs, and—as he
had prayed for them to be—they were all in the one quadrant
of his vision. In one movement, he released Murphy's body
and stood up with the automatic in his hand.

There was a long moment of throbbing, ringing silence as
he faced the four men.

"We can come to an arrangement," Lieutenant Freeborn
said calmly. "I know you're not going to pull that trigger, because you've waited too long. Your type needs to act on the
spur of the moment. What happened just now was unfortunate, I'll admit, but there's no reason why we shouldn't fix up
. . ."

Snook shot him through the stomach, sending the doubled-
up body hurtling against the wall, then wheeled on the three
soldiers who had already begun to flee. Holding the automatic
steady in a two-handed grip, he ranged on the corporal and
squeezed the trigger again. The shot went through the corporal's shoulder, freakishly spinning him round so that he was
facing the way he had come. Snook fired two more shots,
each time seeing the plastic of the corporal's coat flap like a
storm-caught sail, and he held the firing stance until his man
had fallen, until he was certain that no further action was
required of him. The two remaining soldiers disappeared
from view.

All sound and movement ceased.

When humanity eventually returned to Snook, he took a
deep quavering breath and dropped the automatic into his
pocket. Without looking at Murphy again, he walked back to
the area where he had left the group. When he got close they
came forward to meet him, their faces watchful.

"What happened?" Ambrose said. "Where's George?"

Snook kept walking until he was near enough to Quig to
take the brandy bottle from his unresisting fingers. "George
is dead. We ran into Freeborn Junior and three of his men,
and they killed George."

"Oh, *no*," Prudence murmured, and Snook wondered if she had guessed it had been the same group she had met.

"But this can't *be*." Ambrose's face was grim and pale. "Why should they shoot George?"

Snook took a drink from the bottle before he shook his head. "They used a *panga* on George. I did the shooting—with this." He took the automatic from his pocket and held it in the light where it could be seen. His hand was dark with blood.

"Did you hit anybody?" Helig said in a businesslike voice.

Prudence looked at Snook's face. "You did, didn't you?"

He nodded. "I hit Freeborn Junior. And the man who killed George. I hit them square on."

"I don't like the sound of this, old boy. Do you mind?" Helig retrieved his bottle, poured some brandy into a cup and gave the bottle back to Snook. "This place will be swarming with troops in half an hour."

"That's it then," Ambrose said in a dull voice. "It's all over."

"Especially for George."

"I know what you're thinking, Gil—but George Murphy wanted this project to go on."

Snook thought about Murphy, the man with whom he had become friendly only a few days earlier, and was surprised by how little he knew about him. He had no idea where Murphy lived or even if he had any family. All he knew for certain was that Murphy had got himself killed because he was brave and honest, and because he cared about his friends and the miners who worked for him. George Murphy would have liked the transfer project to go on, and the more startling the end result the better, because the greater the world interest that was aroused the less opportunity there would be for force to be used on his miners.

"There might still be time," Snook said. "I don't think young Freeborn and his gang were acting under orders. If it was some kind of a private raid, they mightn't be missed until some time tomorrow."

Helig frowned his doubt. "I wouldn't count on it, old boy.

The guards at the gate are bound to have heard the shooting. Anything could happen."

"Anybody who wants to leave should go now." Ambrose commented, "but I'm staying as long as possible. We could be lucky."

Lucky! Snook thought, wondering just how relative the meaning of a word could become. The brandy bottle was still one-third full and, laying tacit claim to it, he retreated to the same corner where he had stood with Ambrose only ten minutes earlier. Ten minutes was only a short span of time, and yet, because it separated him from a personal epoch in which Murphy had been alive, it could have been years or centuries. His own luck, he now realised, had begun to desert him that day in Malaq three years earlier when he had answered the emergency call to go to the airfield. Looking even more closely at the chain of circumstance, the emergency which had been sparked off by the passing of Thornton's Planet had not been an isolated event. He had quickly forgotten his single look at the livid globe in the sky, but the ancients and today's primitives were wise enough to regard such things as portents of calamities to come. Avernus had suffered at that time, been dragged out of her orbit, and he—without being aware of it—had been caught in the same gravitational maelstrom. Boyce Ambrose, Prudence, George Murphy, Felleth, Curt Freeborn, Helig, Culver, Quig—these were merely the names of asteroids which had been drawn into a deadly spiral, the motive forces of which emanated from another universe.

Looking out into the darkness, taking small regular sips from the bottle, Snook found it hard to credit that astronomy —that most remote and inhuman of the sciences—should have had such a devastating effect on his life. But he was, of course, wrong in thinking of the subject as being remote, especially now that—at points along the equator—the era of close-range astronomy was being ushered in. People could now look at another world from a distance of only a few metres. And in several years' time, when a large crescent of Avernus had emerged through the Earth, astronomy could even become a mass entertainment. It would be possible to stand on a hilltop on a dark night, wearing Amplites, and see the vast luminous dome of the alien planet spanning the horizons and looming high into the sky. The rotation of the Earth would carry watchers closer and closer to the translucent enormity of the planet—revealing details of its land masses, the houses, the people—and finally plunge them under its surface, to emerge some time later on the daylight side, where Avernus would be rendered invisible.

Marshalling unfamiliar thoughts, Snook found, gave him some respite from the anguish he felt over Murphy's death. He tried to visualise the position some thirty-five years ahead when the two worlds were overlapping by only half a planetary diameter. Near the equatorial regions the two great spheres would be intersecting at right angles, in which case the spectators would see a vertical wall sweeping towards them at supersonic speed. On the face of that wall, fountaining upwards into the sky—also at supersonic speed—would be a steady procession of Avernian landmarks seen from directly above. It would require nerve not to close one's eyes at the moment of silent intersection; but a greater spectacle would come thirty-five years beyond that again when the two worlds fully separated from each other. The directions of rotational movement would be opposed to each other at the point of final contact. By that time magniluct glasses might have been improved to the point at which they made Avernus appear completely solid. If so, there would come dizzy, mind-exploding minutes when it would be possible to see the surface of an upside-down world streaming past, just above one's head, at a combined speed of over three thousand kilometres an hour, bombarding the eyesight with inverted buildings and trees which—although insubstantial—would rip through a man's awareness like the teeth on a cosmic circular saw.

And following that, in the year of 2091, would come the ultimate spectacle, with the return of Thornton's Planet.

The separating gap would have increased to less than four thousand kilometres by that time, which meant that—for wearers of Amplites—Avernus would fill the entire sky. Earth would have a ringside seat for the destruction of a world . . .

Snook abruptly pulled back into the present, where he had enough problems of his own. He wondered if the rest of the group, Prudence in particular, understood that he was to die soon. If they did, if she did, no signs were being given to him. He could have done without a show of sympathy from the others, but it would have been good, very good, if Prudence had come to him with words of regret and love, and allowed him to cradle her neat golden head in the crook of his left arm. *Thy navel is like a round goblet, which wanteth not liquor*, the ancient words ran in his mind, *thy belly is like an heap of wheat set about with lilies*.

Thinking back on it, Snook found himself beginning to doubt that the moment of closeness in Prudence's car had actually occurred. Another possibility was that she had responded to him as momentarily and casually as if she had been patting a stray puppy on the head, and with no more meaning. The irony was that he was supposed to have a rare telepathic gift—yet he was less able to divine the workings of a girl's mind than any clumsy adolescent on his first date. Unless one was surrounded by like beings, he decided, telepathy would be an intensifier of loneliness. No apartment is as lonely as the one in which can be heard faint sounds of a party next door.

It occurred to Snook that he was rapidly becoming drunk, but he continued to sip the brandy. A certain degree of intoxication made it easier to accept the fact that there was no way he could get out of Barandi alive. It also made it easier to reach a relevant decision. When Colonel Freeborn came he would be looking for Gilbert Snook—not the other members of the group—and, once he had Snook, he was likely to devote all his attention to him for quite a long time, during which Ambrose might be able to complete the big experiment.

It was a perfectly logical decision, therefore, that—when the Leopards arrived at the mine—he should go forward and give himself up to them.

CHAPTER THIRTEEN

The soldier was so drunk that he would have been unable to stand but for the support of the two military policemen who gripped his arms. From the state of his uniform it was obvious that he had fallen more than once, and had been helplessly sick. In spite of his physical misery, he was terrified in the presence of Colonel Tommy Freeborn, and he told his story in disconnected groups of words—with frequent lapses into Swahili—which made sense only to someone who had already the general picture. When he had finished speaking, the Colonel stared at him with leaden-eyed contempt.

"You're positive," Freeborn said, after a pause, "that it was the white man, Snook, who had the weapon?"

"Yes, sir." The soldier's head rolled from side to side as he spoke. "And I only done what the Lieutenant told me."

"Take this object away," Freeborn ordered. As the redcaps bundled the soldier out of the office, the sergeant who accompanied them glanced back with an unspoken question. Freeborn nodded and mimed the action of pulling a hat down over his ears. The sergeant—who was a useful man, and knew that the invisible hat was a polythene bag—saluted correctly and left the office.

As soon as he was alone, Colonel Freeborn lowered his head and thought for a few moments about his brother's son, then he opened a communicator channel and gave a series of orders which would assemble a force of a hundred men at the entrance to National Mine No. 3. He picked up his cane, flicked a speck of dust from his half-sleeved shirt, and, walking with a firm and measured tread went outside to where his car was waiting. It was two hours before dawn and the night wind was cold, but he waved away the coat offered by his driver and got into the car's rear seat.

During the drive from Kisumu he sat without moving, bare arms folded, and in his mind apportioned the blame for his nephew's death. One part he allocated to himself—in his efforts to eradicate Curt's weaknesses he had pushed the boy too much; a larger portion he laid at the door of Paul Ogilvie, without whose interference there would have been no unwanted foreigners meddling with the operation of the mine; but the greatest share of the guilt lay with the insolent trickster, Gilbert Snook, who should have been put down like a dog on the day he entered Barandi.

The hour was not yet ripe for Ogilvie to be brought to book, but within a short time—a very short time, Freeborn promised himself—Snook would regret that he had not been quietly suffocated three years earlier. Each thought of Snook was like the opening of a furnace door within Freeborn's head, and as he neared the mine he could feel himself being buoyed higher and higher on the searing blasts. It was like a plunge into black Arctic waters, therefore, when—on reaching the mine entrance—he saw one of the Presidential limousines parked outside the gates. Its gleaming waxy haunches looked incongruous against the backdrop of military trucks and watchful troops. He got out of his own car and, knowing what was required of him, went straight to the limousine and got into the rear seat beside Paul Ogilvie.

The President did not turn his head as he spoke. "I want an explanation for this, Tommy."

"The situation has changed since we . . ." Uncharacteristically, Freeborn abandoned his officialese. "Curt has been murdered by Snook."

"I've heard about that. I'm still waiting for an explanation of why these men are here."

"But—" Freeborn felt his temples begin to throb. "I've just told you—my nephew has been murdered."

"Telling me that your nephew and other members of his regiment went into the mine against my orders does not explain why you have assembled this force of men here against my orders." Ogilvie's voice was dry and cold. "Are you challenging my authority?"

"I would never do that," Freeborn said, flooding his voice with sincerity, while his mind weighed up the kind of factors which influence the history of nations. His service automatic was within reach of his right hand, but before he could use it he would have to open the leather flap of its holster. It was most unlikely that Ogilvie would have ventured out without protection, and yet he must have moved very quickly after being contacted by his informants. This moment, here in the darkness of the car, could be a pivotal point for the whole of Barandi—and Curt's death might have served a useful purpose . . .

"A penny for them." The note of complacency in Ogilvie's voice told Freeborn all he needed to know. The President was protected, and the *status quo* would have to remain for some time yet.

"Leaving personal issues aside," Freeborn said, "the Leopard Regiment is a keystone of our internal security. Those men out there don't know anything about international policies and diplomacies—what they *do* know is that two of their comrades have been shot down in cold blood by a white foreigner. They don't think very much about anything, but if they get the idea that such actions are not followed by swift punishment . . ."

"You don't need to spell it out for me, Tommy. But the UN people will be here tomorrow."

"And will they be favourably impressed to learn that murderers go unpunished in Barandi?" Sensing he had found the right approach, Freeborn pressed home his argument. "I'm not proposing a massacre of innocents, Paul. The only man I want is Snook, and he's probably an embarrassment to the others—they'll probably be glad to get rid of him."

"What are you proposing?"

"Let me go in there with a couple of men and simply ask that he give himself up. I'd only have to hint that it would be for the benefit of the others. Including the girl."

"You think it would be enough?"

"I think it would be enough," Freeborn said. "You see, Snook is that kind of a fool."

Having disposed of the brandy, Snook climbed up on the platform and watched the others at work. Since hearing of

Murphy's death they had gone about their tasks with a moody determination, only speaking when necessary. Ambrose, Culver and Quig spent most of their time kneeling at the complex control panel on the rear surface of the Moncaster machine. Even Helig and Prudence were busy with hammers and nails, erecting a makeshift handrail which Ambrose had decreed necessary for safety reasons. They had already completed another structure resembling a shower cubicle built of wood and clear plastic sheeting. Two cylinders of hydrogen stood inside the transparent box.

The concerted activity, in which he had no part, increased Snook's sense of not belonging, and it was almost with relief that he heard the distant growl of truck engines.

None of the others appeared to notice the sound, so he did not mention it. Minutes dragged by without any sign of military activity, and he began to wonder if his imagination had conjured with the irregular soughing of the night wind. The logical thing, bearing in mind the decision he had reached, would have been to stroll quietly towards the mine entrance, but he felt a powerful reluctance simply to fade away into the darkness. He was not of the group, and yet he did not want to face the alternative.

"That's it." Ambrose stood up and rubbed his hands together. "The mini-pile is delivering all the power we need. I think we're all set." He glanced at his watch. "Less than half an hour to go."

"That's quite a machine," Snook said, suddenly aware of the enormity of what was being attempted.

"It certainly is. Up until ten years ago you would have needed an accelerator about five kilometres long to produce the radiation fields we can make right in here." Ambrose stroked the top of the machine as if it were a favourite pet.

"Isn't it dangerous?"

"It can be if you stand in front of it, but that applies to a bicycle as well. It's machines like this that have speeded up nuclear research so much in the last decade—and with what we're learning from Felleth . . .

"Watch out for the cubicle!" Ambrose shouted to Helig.

"We can't afford any rips in the plastic skin—it has to be air-tight."

Snook examined the flimsy structure with growing doubt. "Is that where you're expecting Felleth to materialise?"

"That's the place."

"But will he have to stay in there? How do you know he breathes hydrogen?"

"The hydrogen isn't for breathing, Gil. It's to provide the physical environment Felleth specified for his arrival, or part of it anyway. His knowledge is away beyond mine, but I think it's to provide a convenient supply of protons which he'll use to . . ."

"Doctor Ambrose," bellowed an amplified voice from the encircling blackness. "This is Colonel Freeborn, Head of Barandian Internal Security. Can you hear me?"

Snook moved towards the ladder, but Ambrose gripped his arm with surprising strength. "I can hear you, Colonel."

"This afternoon President Ogilvie sent instructions that you were to stop working here. Did you receive the message?"

"I received it."

"Then why are you disobeying?"

Ambrose hesitated. "I'm not disobeying, Colonel. One of these machines has a miniature nuclear reactor inside it, and the controls aren't working properly. We've spent the last six hours trying to close it down."

"That sounds like a very convenient story, Doctor Ambrose."

"If you'd like to come up here I'll show you what I mean."

"I'm prepared to let it pass for the time being," Freeborn's voice boomed. "I see that you have Snook with you."

"Yes—Mister Snook is here."

"I have come to place him under arrest for the murder of two members of the Barandian Armed Forces."

"For *what?*" Ambrose's voice was hoarse with the effort of shouting.

"I think you heard me, Doctor."

"Yes, but it was so unexpected that I . . . We did hear some shooting, but I had no idea what was happening. This is terrible." Ambrose released Snook's arm and backed away from him.

"The reason I'm keeping my distance is that Snook is armed. It will not prevent his arrest, of course, but I would prefer that he be taken without any shooting. I have no wish for the innocent members of your party to be hurt, and that can be avoided if Snook will give himself up."

"Thank you, Colonel." Ambrose's shadowed face was unreadable as he stared at Snook. "You'll appreciate that this has come as a great shock to me and the other members of my party who, as you say, are innocent and had no idea of what was going on. May we have a little time to talk things over?"

"Fifteen minutes—no more."

A lengthy silence ensued, showing that Freeborn considered the dialogue to have ended.

"Nice work, Boyce," Snook said, keeping his voice low in case remote listening devices were trained on him. He recognised that Ambrose had acted with superb common sense in dissociating himself and the others, but the knowledge did not ease his irrational sense of betrayal. He nodded to Prudence and the three other men, and turned to leave.

"Gil," Ambrose whispered fiercely, "where in the hell do you think you're going?"

"In hell? Any old place will do."

"Stay right there. I'm going to get you out of this."

Snook gave a humourless laugh. "There's no way out. Besides, the little diversion could give you enough time to complete the experiment. That's the main item on the agenda, isn't it?"

Ambrose shook his head. "We agreed earlier tonight that I'm a self-centred bastard, but I have to draw the line somewhere. I don't mind admitting I was hoping to be left alone long enough to go ahead as planned, but now the situation has changed."

"Look . . ." Snook tapped himself on the chest. "I don't want to sound melodramatic, but I'm as good as dead already. There's nothing you can do about it."

"I know you're as good as dead, Gil," Ambrose said, his voice resonant. "Otherwise I wouldn't risk offering you the one escape that's available."

"Escape?" Snook felt the same old chill of premonition as he glanced at the cubical machine. "Where to?"

"There's nowhere else for you to go," Ambrose replied. "Nowhere except . . . Avernus."

☆

Snook took an involuntary step backwards, then looked around the rest of the group standing close by. Their faces were solemn and wide-eyed, like those of children, attention directed towards Ambrose.

"There's a risk involved," Ambrose said. "I can only do this with your consent and co-operation, and I wouldn't try it at all if you had any other hope of getting out of here."

Snook swallowed painfully. "What would you do?"

"There just isn't time to give you a course in nuclear physics, Gil. Basically it involves reversing Felleth's processes, making you neutron-rich—but you'll just have to trust me. Are you willing?"

"I'm willing," Snook said. He glimpsed in his mind's eye the elongated diamond-shapes of Avernian islands. "But it isn't what you came here to do."

"That doesn't matter. In this situation I couldn't risk transferring Felleth, or any other Avernian, into our universe—somebody would probably shoot him." Ambrose paused to light a cigarette, his gaze locked on Snook's face. "But we can still prove the principle of operation, for Felleth's benefit."

"All right." Snook discovered he was more afraid than he had been at the prospect of merely being killed. "What do you want me to do?"

"Well, the first thing you have to do is get in touch with Felleth and tell him about the change of plan."

"Boyce, you make it sound . . . Have you got his phone number?"

"He'll need reaction time, Gil. He has a lot of expertise, but even so he'll need some warning so that he can make ready to receive you." Ambrose's face was impassive, but Snook sensed that his brain was racing, evaluating probabilities like a world-class card player.

"Do you think he can do it in time?" Snook knew the question demanded resources of knowledge which did not exist on Earth, but was unable to hold it back.

"Felleth is way ahead of us in this field, and the energy relationships favour a transfer from this universe into his. I think that with him doing a lot of pulling, and us doing a bit of pushing, it should work out all right."

Snook suddenly realised he had lost all human contact with Ambrose—it was impossible to tell whether he was giving reassurance as a friend, or taking the appropriate action to protect his experiment. It made no practical difference either way—his own choice was between the certainty of death on Earth and the possibility of life on Avernus. He turned towards Prudence, but she looked away from him immediately, and he knew at once that she was afraid. A fresh worry appeared in his mind.

"Boyce, supposing everything works out right and I sort of . . . disappear," he said, "what's going to happen here afterwards? Freeborn isn't going to like it very much."

Ambrose was unperturbed. "That problem will take care of itself—but you're not even going to have a chance to transfer unless you do something about contacting Felleth right now." He examined his watch, clicking its display buttons. "He'll be coming up through the station we marked on Level Two in just over four minutes."

"I'll go," Snook said quietly, aware that the time for talking had passed.

They went down the ladder and assembled in a tight group beneath the platform, giving cover for Snook as he slipped away towards the mine head. He ran as quickly as possible, depending on the blue lenses of his Amplites to keep him from falling over obstacles, and praying that Freeborn had not taken the precaution of saturating the area with his men. It came to him that Freeborn had been strangely gentle in his handling of the situation, but there was not time for analysis of his motives.

Nearing the entrance of the shaft, he remained as long as possible in the lee of the vacuum pipes which curved away from it like the tentacles of a huge octopus. By repeating the moves that Murphy had always made, he started the elevator machinery and was grateful for the silence of its operation. He stepped into a descending cage, rode it downwards to Level Two and leaped out on to the circular gallery. For a panicky moment he was unable to identify the opening of the south pipe, then he was inside it and running with the cold air sighing in his ears.

When he reached the area marked out by Ambrose he found that Felleth and several other Avernians were already present, visible from the waist up above the rock floor, and coming more fully into view with every second, their unnaturally wide mouths pouting and pursing. The bluish translucent figures were interspersed with what seemed to be machines and tall rectangular cabinets.

None of the Avernians reacted to his arrival, and Snook recalled that on this occasion he was not being illuminated for them by Ambrose's special equipment. He fixed his gaze on Felleth—one part of his mind wondering how he had made the identification—and went forward. Felleth suddenly raised his web-fingered hands to his head, and Snook saw the glint of the living green wall superimposed on his vision. He inclined his head towards Felleth's, once more seeing the mist-pools of the eyes grow larger and larger until they swamped his mind.

> Deep peace of the running wave.
> I understand you, Equal Gil. You may come.
> Deep peace of the running wave.

Snook found himself kneeling on the uneven wet stone of the tunnel floor, his Amplites showing—apart from a view of his normal surroundings—only a vague general radiance. That meant, he remembered, that the surface of Avernus had already risen above his head. He looked up at the curving hewn roof, wondering how much time he had lost. If he was to have any chance of life he had to rendezvous with Felleth and Ambrose at a point directly above his present position. Felleth was already on his way, straight up through geological strata which, for him, were non-existent—but for Snook there was no option other than retracing his steps.

He got to his feet, trying to throw off the now-familiar weakness which followed telepathic union, and ran towards the shaft. Reaching the gallery, he climbed into an ascending cage and clung to its mesh sides until he had been carried up to ground level. He lowered his head and ran towards the platform, heedless now of anyone trying to stop him. The portable lights surrounding the platform came into view in the starless black, and with the sight there returned his appreciation of the need to avoid blundering into possible enemies. He slowed his pace, crouched low and silently made his way to the base of the platform. Ambrose and Helig were waiting for him at the foot of the ladder.

"I got to Felleth," Snook blurted, fighting to control his breathing. "It's all right."

"Good work," Ambrose said. "We'd better go up and get started. There isn't much time."

They climbed the ladder and found Prudence and the other three men standing in a silent group. Snook got the impression they had been holding a whispered conversation and had broken it off on his arrival. There was a strong feeling of embarrassment, none of them wanting to meet his gaze, and he knew that barriers had fallen into place in the same way as when it is learned that a member of a family or group is going to die. No matter how hard they may try, he realised, people who know they have a continuing future cannot help being alienated by the aura surrounding a person who is making ready to die. In theory, Snook's life was being saved by nuclear magic—but his world-line was about to be terminated with a finality equal to that of the grave, and the fact had to be subconsciously resented by all others present.

"We don't need this," Ambrose said, pushing the plastic hydrogen tent out of the way. He upended a small wooden crate where the tent had been. "You'd better sit on this, Gil."

"Right." Snook tried to appear stolid and unmoved, but a deathly chill had gathered inside him, and his knees felt weak as he crossed the platform and shook hands with Helig,

Culver and Quig. He had no idea why the formality suddenly seemed necessary to him. Prudence took his hand in both of hers, but her face was the mask of a high priestess as he kissed her once, very lightly and very briefly. He was turning away when she spoke his name.

He said, "What is it, Prudence?" There flickered in him the hope that she would give him something, a gift of words, to take to another world.

"I . . ." her voice was almost inaudible. "I'm sorry I laughed at your name."

He nodded his head, strangely gratified and unable to speak, then went and sat down on the crate. The only occasion on which Prudence had shown amusement over his name had been at their very first meeting, and in his state of abject craving for human comfort it seemed to him that the odd apology had been her way of wiping clean the slate of subsequent events. *That's as good as you're going to get*, he thought. *Perhaps it was more than you could have expected, under the circumstances.* He looked all around him, taking in the sight which—barring some grotesque anticlimax—was to be his last view of Earth.

The five people on the platform stared back at him, but their blue-lenses Amplite glasses—which enabled them to see in darkness—made them look like blind people. Surrounding the crude wooden stage was a curtain of night which was now beginning to abate slightly, and he knew that dawn was near. Only the thick covering of low cloud, similar to that of Avernus, was keeping the level of light so low. Ambrose had moved in behind the Moncaster machine and was intent on its controls when Freeborn's voice crashed from out of the blackness.

"The fifteen minutes is up, Doctor," it said, "and I'm tired of waiting."

"We haven't finished our discussion," Ambrose shouted, his hands still busy.

"What is there to discuss?"

"You must understand that it's asking a lot for us to hand over a man when we have no evidence of his crime."

"You've been playing games with me, Doctor." The

amplification and echoes made Freeborn's voice come from all sides at once. "You'll be sorry you did that. If Snook doesn't give himself up immediately I'm coming to take him."

The words brought it home to Snook that, regardless of what might have lain in store for him, he was still an inhabitant of Earth and retained all his responsibilities. "I have to go down there, Boyce," he said. "We've run out of time."

"Stay where you are," Ambrose commanded. "Kill the lights, Des." Quig stooped and pulled a cable connection apart, and the faint light reflecting upwards from the ring of ground lights abruptly vanished.

"What good will that do?" Snook half-rose, then sank back on to his improvised seat. With the onset of full darkness, ghostly blue fingers could be seen beyond the edge of the platform. The inhabitants of Avernus—silent, translucent and awesome—moved among and through the piles of dank lumber, their eyes turning without seeing, their wide mouths moving without speech. In a few seconds there came the cries of frightened men. A gun was fired time after time, but the shots were not directed at human targets, and eventually there was a return to silence. The Avernians continued their strolling, unaware of anything outside their own universe.

"I was sure we could buy some time that way," Ambrose said, secure in his role of master magician as the faint outlines of a building became visible about him. "Now, Gil, this is it. Felleth will be up level with us in a couple of minutes, and I've got to get you ready for him."

With the removal of one danger, Snook's former fears returned to him and he sought the comfort of words again. "What are you going to do to me, Boyce?" An instinct prompted him to take the automatic from his pocket and slide it away from him across the uneven timber.

"I'm surrounding you with a flux of neutrons, that's all." Ambrose sounded calm. "I'm making you neutron-rich."

Incredibly, Snook found he was still capable of thought. "But parts of a nuclear plant are bombarded with neutrons for years, and they just stay put. Don't they?"

"It isn't the same thing, Gil. In a power plant the neutrons don't exist long enough, or else they're manifested in other reactions." Ambrose went on speaking in the same reassuring monotone as the figures of Felleth and other Avernians and their equipment rose up around him. "This is mainly Felleth's show, of course—he's got all the work of synthesising your body with his elements. All we know is that the free neutrons to which you're being converted will decay into protons, electrons and anti-neutrons. And Felleth will ensure that the anti-neutrinos are preserved . . ."

Snook ceased listening to the incantation as the insubstantial framework of a cabinet was manoeuvred into place around him by Avernians who had luminous mist-pools for eyes. He looked for Prudence, but she had covered her face with her hands. There was just enough time for him to hope that she was crying for his sake . . .

Then he journeyed beyond the stars.

CHAPTER FOURTEEN

The room was about ten metres square, but seemed smaller because of the amount of equipment it contained—and because of the presence of the Avernians.

Snook looked at them in silence, without trying to move, while his body recovered from the sensation of having been *jolted*. He was breathing normally, and his physical functions seemed to be continuing as they always did, but his nerves felt as though they were vibrating in the aftermath of a paralysing shock, like tunnels in which there lingered the echoes of a scream.

The Avernians stared back at him with brooding concentration, also in silence, their eyes watchful. Snook discovered that his growing familiarity with their general appearance as seen from Earth, the sketches in luminous mist, had not prepared him for the solid, three-dimensional reality. In previous encounters he had been impressed by their similarity to human beings; now he was in a room with them, breathing the same air, and his overwhelming impression was one of alienation.

One part of his mind felt a numb gratitude over the fact that he was alive, but with each passing second that consideration seemed less and less important, or even relevant. The only truth which retained any significance was that he was alone in a world peopled by unknown and unknowable beings whose eyes and noses were clustered too close to the tops of their heads, and whose mouths twitched and pursed and flowed with frightening mobility. The skin of the Avernians shaded from a pale yellow around the eyes and mouths to a coppery brown at the hands and feet, and had a waxy sheen to it. They were surrounded by an unnameable odour, suggestive of formaldehyde and perhaps cardamom, which added to their strangeness and caused an upward lift of Snook's stomach muscles.

Five seconds gone—thirty years to go, he thought, and with the thought came claustrophobic panic. *Why doesn't Felleth speak? Why doesn't he help me?*

"I have been . . . talking to you, Equal Gil," Felleth said in a laboured, husking voice. "We have an unfortunate situation . . . we have access to your mind . . . but we are screened from yours . . . and you would not wish for me . . . to come closer."

"No!" Snook jumped to his feet and stood swaying. His shoulder struck an open-fronted cabinet which had been enclosing him on three sides and it rolled backwards on castors. He looked down and saw that the wooden box on which he had been sitting was itself resting on an irregularly shaped section of wet timber which contrasted with the polished white floor beneath it. The words, JENNINGS ALES, stencilled on the side of the box might have been chosen for their homeliness, as a reminder that everything he knew had been left on the far side of infinity.

"I have to go back," he said. "Send me back Felleth. Anywhere on Earth."

"That is not possible . . . energy relationships not favourable . . . no receiving station for you." Felleth's chest heaved, apparently from the strain of reproducing human speech. "You need time . . . to adjust."

"I can't adjust. You don't know . . ."

"We do know . . . we have access . . . we know that we are . . . repellent to you."

"I can't help that."

"Try to remember . . . you impose greater strain on us . . . we have access . . . and you have killed."

Snook looked at the robed figures of the Avernians, and there came a glimmer of understanding of the fact that they had needed courage to remain in the same room with him. The Avernians, he recalled, were a gentle, pacific race, and this particular group were bound to feel that they had conjured up a dangerous primitive. He glanced instinctively at his right hand and saw that it still bore traces of George Murphy's blood. His xenophobia began to be swept aside by a sense of shame.

"I'm sorry," Snook said.

"I think it is important that you should rest . . . to recover from the mental and physical effects . . . of the transfer." The breath whistled and sighed in Felleth's throat as he vocalised the words being taken from Snook's mind. "This is not a dwelling place . . . but we have prepared a bed . . . in the adjoining apartment . . . follow me." Felleth walked with a stately gliding movement to a doorless opening which was narrower at the top than at the floor level.

Snook gazed after him for a few seconds without stirring. The notion of falling asleep was ludicrous, then he understood he was being given the chance to be alone. He started after Felleth, then turned, picked up the beer crate and took it with him. Felleth led the way along a short corridor which, at the far end, had a window giving a view of grey sky and grey ocean growing lighter with dawn. Snook followed his guide into a small room containing nothing but a simple couch. The room had a single window and the walls were decorated with horizontal strips of neutral colour, seemingly in a random pattern.

"We will meet again," Felleth said. "And you will feel better."

Snook nodded, still holding the crate, and waited until Felleth withdrew. The doorway was of the same trapezoid shape as the first, but vertical leaves slid from recesses in the wall to seal it. Snook went to the window and looked out at the world which was to be his home. There was a descending vista of brown-tiled roofs, with occasional views of alleys and squares in which the People could be seen going about their unhurried, enigmatic affairs. They wore flowing, draped garments of white or blue, and from a distance they resembled citizens of ancient Greece. There were no vehicles in sight, no light standards or telephone poles, no antennae.

The ocean began without intervention of open land, stretching to the horizon, and a hundred islands were ranged across it like ships at anchor. Most of the islands rose to central low peaks, creating—with their reflections—elongated diamond-shapes, but in the middle distance a pair were made into one by a massive double-spanned arch. Snook had seen it before, in a vision implanted by Felleth.

He turned away from the window, his mind sated with strangeness, and went to the couch. He placed the orange-dyed wooden crate beside it, then took off his wrist watch and set it on top, establishing his own little island of the commonplace. Next, he removed his blue raincoat—which was still spattered with the moisture of Earth—rolled it up and placed it beside the crate. When he lay down he discovered an unutterable weariness coiling through his limbs, but it was a long time before he escaped into sleep.

Snook had a dream that he was with Prudence Devonald, and that they were shopping for coffee and cheese in a small-town store. Beyond the gold-lettered store windows was a busy high street, with red buses, a church spire and leaves scattering in an October breeze. The gem-like clarity of the dream made it very real, the simple happiness he felt was very real, and when it began to slip away he fought to hold on, because the tiny part of him which was not deceived told him the awakening would be bad.

It was.

He sat on the edge of the couch, with head lowered, then the mental habits of a lifetime began to reassert themselves.

Boy meets girl, boy loses girl, he thought. *Boy has to find out if there's any plumbing in this place.*

He stood up, looked around the bare room and picked up his watch, which told him it was past noon. The increased brightness from the single window confirmed what he already knew, that Avernian time kept pace with that of Earth. He went to the door and tried to slide the two leaves apart, but they refused to move, and the central crack was too narrow to give his fingers any purchase. The idea that he had been locked in did not cross his mind—he was certain the door could be opened easily by anyone who knew what to do, and therefore he was reluctant to call for help. He tried moving around on the floor near the threshold, testing for pressure switches, then a tentative solution occurred to him. Blanking everything else from his thoughts, he walked steadily and confidently towards the door, *expecting* it to open.

The leaves parted at once and, before he had time to think about what was happening, he was outside in the corridor. He looked back at the opening in appreciative wonderment, revising his ideas about Avernian technology. Remarks passed by Ambrose had told him that Felleth and his co-workers were ahead of Earth in their understanding of nuclear physics, but Snook had formed an opinion that on Avernus advanced knowledge was stored rather than applied. His one view of the island he was on had reinforced his notion of a non-technical culture, but his judgements as a newcomer obviously were not valid, his eyes not adequate. Perhaps a patch of colour on a wall could be the equivalent of a heating system; perhaps a wall stone that was rounded instead of squared was a power receiver and distributor.

Snook walked to the end of the corridor and went down a short flight of stairs which had awkward proportions and sloping treads which gave him the feeling he was going to pitch forward. At the bottom was a much larger room than any he had been in, though—like the one in which he had slept—it was devoid of furnishings. The windows along two walls were of obscured glass, but the movement of shrub-like vegetation beyond them told him he was at ground level. There were patches of lighter colour on the greenish stone floor which suggested that objects had recently been removed, and he recalled Felleth's statement that the building was not a dwelling. Questions began to well up in Snook's mind. Was it a store? A library? What had the Avernian upstairs thought when he had first seen Snook appear in the little room a week earlier?

A door opened in one of the end walls and Felleth entered the room, his large pale eyes fixed on Snook. For an instant, superimposed on his normal vision, Snook seemed to glimpse the rise and sparkling fall of a translucent green wave, and—without speaking—he tried to coax the image into sharp focus, thinking of the ocean as a symbol of tranquillity and endless power.

"I believe you will learn to hear and speak," Felleth said in his laboured whisper.

"Thank you." Snook felt gratified, then realised his acceptance of his new situation must be growing if he could respond with positive emotion towards a vaguely saurian biped in classical Mediterranean dress.

"Toilet facilities have been prepared for you." Felleth indicated a second door with a gesture of a webbed hand. "They are self-enclosed . . . and therefore not of the highest standard . . . but it is only for a short period."

Snook was baffled for a moment, then understanding came. "Of course," he said, "I'm in quarantine."

"Only for a short period."

It dawned on Snook that, in his urgent need to get out of Barandi alive, he had unthinkingly accepted a great many things about conditions on Avernus. The atmosphere, for instance, could have been of a mix which was totally unacceptable for human beings, and its micro-organisms could already be setting up deadly colonies in his lungs. Presumably, he could represent a medical risk to the Avernians, which might explain why the building he was in had a scoured-out feel to it.

"I would not have brought you here . . . if I had not been satisfied you would live," Felleth responded to his thought. "In any case, I could have provided . . . breathing gases and a mask."

"You think of everything." Snook was reminded of the fact that Felleth was the Avernian equivalent of a leading philosopher/scientist.

"Not everything. There are important matters we must discuss . . . while you are eating."

After Snook had made use of the receptacles and water supply provided for him within a polished metal cubicle, he joined Felleth in another room containing a table and a simple stool which seemed to have been newly made from close-grained wood. On the table were ceramic platters of vegetables, cereals and fruit, plus a flask of water. Snook sat down at once, suddenly conscious that he had not eaten for a long time, and tried the food. The flavours were strange, though not unpleasant, his main criticism being that everything—even the fruit and green vegetables—had a tang of iodine and salt.

"I have to advise you, Equal Gil," Felleth began, "that in bringing you here I miscalculated in certain matters . . . and failed to consider others at all."

"That doesn't sound like you, Felleth." Snook had considered simply thinking his replies to the Avernian's remarks, but he found that speaking aloud called for less mental effort.

"At present I am not in good standing . . . with my fellow Responders . . . nor with the People . . . because I gave them advice in an important matter . . . without investigating all the evidence available to me."

"I don't understand."

"For example . . . I accepted, uncritically, everything I learned about astronomy . . . from your mind."

Snook looked up at the enigmatic, robed figure. "That doesn't seem like a blunder to me. After all, you'd only just heard of the subject, and on Earth they've had astronomy for thousands of years."

"On Earth—that is precisely the point . . . your astronomers study a different universe."

"I still don't get it." Snook pushed his food aside, sensing that something important was coming.

"The picture they presented of my universe . . . contained only those elements of which they had become aware . . . a sun, this world . . . and the rogue world you call Thornton's Planet."

"So?"

"The orbit they calculated for Thornton's Planet . . . was based on this simplistic universe-picture."

"I'm sorry, Felleth—I'm not an astronomer and I still don't see what you are getting at."

Felleth came closer to the table. "You are not an astronomer . . . but you understand that all bodies in a planetary system . . . are influenced in their movements . . . by all other bodies in that system."

"That's elementary," Snook said. "But if there aren't any other bodies in the . . ." He stopped speaking as the full implication of Felleth's words dawned on him. "Have they begun to look?"

"A radio telescope has been designed . . . and at least twenty will be built."

"But this is *good*." Snook stood up to face Felleth. "This gives you hope, doesn't it? I mean, if you can find just one other planet prowling around out there, it could pull Thornton's Planet off the collision course . . ."

"That is what I should have appreciated . . . at once."

"How could you?"

"The People demand the highest standards of a Responder . . . it is their right."

"But . . ."

"Equal Gil, your memory is imperfect by our standards . . . but it may contain information which would enable me to make restitution to the People . . . for my failure . . . please permit me to touch you."

Snook hesitated only briefly before stepping closer to Felleth. He inclined his head forward, and kept his eyes open while Felleth closed with him and their foreheads touched. The contact lasted only a second, then Felleth stepped back.

"Thank you," Felleth said. "The evidence is valuable."

"I didn't feel anything—what evidence?"

"When you first heard of Thornton's Planet . . . it was expected to pass through your world . . . but it missed by many planetary diameters . . . and the divergence from the predicted course . . . was attributed to observational error."

"I do seem to remember something about . . ." Snook's excitement increased. "That's evidence, isn't it? It shows there are other planets in your own system."

"Not conclusive evidence."

"It seems conclusive to me."

"The only positive conclusion," Felleth said, "is that I am unworthy of the People's trust."

"That's ridiculous," Snook almost shouted. "They owe you everything."

The long slit of Felleth's mouth rippled in an emotional signal which Snook could not interpret. "The People have different mental attributes to those of your race . . . but they are not superior, as you believe . . . we have successfully rid ourselves of the great destructive passions . . . but it is more difficult to eradicate the trivial and the petty . . . the fact that I am using the words indicates that I, too . . ." Felleth broke off from the painful manufacture of speech sounds, his pale eyes locked on Snook's in an oddly human display of helplessness. Snook stared at him in silence, then ideas began to crystallise and dissolve far back in his consciousness.

"Felleth," he said, "is there something you have to tell me?"

Each day passed like a month; each month like a year.

Snook found that the small island allocated to him was sufficient for his needs, provided he worked hard with the simple agricultural tools which had been supplied, and regularly culled the shallows for edible sea plants. He had no tobacco or alcohol—the processes of fermentation were not used on Avernus outside science laboratories—but he had learned to live without them. The Avernians themselves, he knew, sometimes inhaled the vapours released from the pods of certain marine plants, claiming they had the power to elevate the spirit and enrich the vision. In the beginning, Snook had experimented with the pods, but always with negative results, and had concluded that his metabolism was wrong. "It may be a universal law," he had written on a scrap of paper, "that you can only get high at home."

When he was not busy with the growing of food, Snook had enough work of other kinds with which to occupy his time. The island's only house had to be kept in repair—especially the roof—and he also had to mend his own clothes and shoes. Heating was no problem, because the stone slabs of the floor grew warm at night, apparently spontaneously. Snook almost wished that the heating was of a more primitive nature—a log fire would have given him companionship of a kind. It would have been especially appreciated in the dark evenings when he had been incautious enough to start thinking of Prudence, and the lights of the other islands reminded him that the life of the planet was continuing without his aid.

There is no apartment so lonely, he recalled his own thought, *as the one in which can be heard faint sounds of a party next door.*

Being a prisoner on a small uninhabited island added little to the tribulations of being a prisoner in an alien universe, Snook had learned, even though the People had proved themselves much more human than he had expected. With Felleth as his sole model, he had formed an idealised impression of the Avernians—the super-intelligent beings who were rebuilding their civilisation after one planet-wide disaster, and were stoically preparing themselves for the ultimate calamity.

It had come as a shock to him to discover that the race of reason-guided beings resented his presence on their world as a representative of a sister planet which was refusing them a helping hand. And he had been both saddened and angered to learn that Felleth had been permanently censured for having failed, as the Avernians saw it, in his duty as a Responder. They had also criticised Felleth for his unilateral action in transferring Snook into their world.

"It is more difficult," Felleth had said, on the first day, "to eradicate the trivial and the petty."

These were things which Snook tried not to think about as he struggled with his own burden—that of enduring from one day to the next, then repeating the process over and over again. Living in a world where nobody wanted to kill him was one thing; but the reverse of the coin was that he existed in a universe in which nobody had given him life and where there was no prospect of his passing life on to others. The thoughts were painful for a man with his particular history, for a human neutrino, but then he had realised his mistake the day he had walked into a hotel in Kisumu and had seen . . .

At that point in the evening Snook always went through the ritual of taking off his wrist watch and placing it on the orange-dyed crate beside his bed. And—if he had worked hard enough that day—he was blessed with sleep, sometimes with dreams.

Each day passed like a month; each month like a year.

CHAPTER FIFTEEN

Twelve months had passed, by Snook's reckoning, on the morning he received the wordless message that the Avernians had confirmed the existence of other worlds in their own planetary system.

His early experiences on Avernus had shown that his facility for mind-to-mind communication was not much greater than it had been when he had lived on Earth and occasionally had snared the thoughts of other men. Ironically, he had been able to achieve full congruency of self with Felleth only when they had inhabited different universes and had been able to merge their brains in the same volume of space. During Felleth's regular visits to the island he had tried to extend his ability to receive data, but progress had been uncertain if it existed at all.

On this special day, however, he could not fail to be aware of the mood of the People. The emotions of joy and triumph, amplified millions of times, were spangled across the islands like the gold of the sunsets they never saw.

"Not bad," Snook said aloud, looking up from his digging.

"From complete ignorance of the skies to fully-fledged radio astronomy in one year. Not bad."

He returned his attention to the work in hand, but kept scanning the waterways in the hope that Felleth would pay him a special visit to bring details of the new knowledge. The masses and orbital elements of the other worlds would determine the distance by which Thornton's Planet would miss Avernus on its next pass, and Snook felt a proprietory interest in the information. He was incapable of understanding the relevant sets of equations, but they had affected the whole course of his life, and he wanted to know whether Avernus was destined for another disaster, of greater or lesser proportions, or if it had been granted a total reprieve. It also occurred to him that the People might regard his presence among them less distasteful were they assured of their futures once more.

Should that prove to be the case, he would ask for the right to travel as freely as he had once done on Earth. Felleth had told him there were larger land masses to the west and east, and exploring them—perhaps circumnavigating the watery globe—might give his life a semblance of purpose.

No boat came near him that day, but when darkness fell he saw a profusion of coloured lights on the other islands which told him that celebrations were in progress. He watched the moving specks of brilliance for several hours before going to bed, wondering if it was another universal law that at times of happiness and victory sentient beings would express their feelings with pyrotechnics, the symbols of cosmic birth.

On the following morning a fleet of four boats passed the island at high speed, heading north-east. Snook, who could not recall seeing craft go in that directon before, watched them with some puzzlement. They were of a type powered by sophisticated batteries—in which the sea itself served as an electrolyte—and therefore had virtually unlimited range, but he had no knowledge of land on that particular bearing.

When the little fleet was at its nearest to him, a white-clad figure waved to Snook from the leading boat. He waved back, pleased for a moment by the simple act of communication, then began to wonder if the anonymous figure had been

Felleth, and why he should be speeding off into an empty ocean. Within minutes the four boats had dwindled to invisibility on the flat grey waters.

In spite of several rain showers, Snook remained outside all that day, but did not see the boats return. By the following day the incident was fading from his mind, and he remained indoors concentrating on the task of constructing an earthenware oven from local clay. The Avernians were not only strictly vegetarian—they ate all their food in its natural state, and Felleth had not felt obliged to provide Snook with cooking facilities. He had adapted reasonably well to living on raw food, but lately had become obsessed with the idea of making hot soups. A doubly cherished ambition was that of grinding cereal, baking it into bread and serving it to himself with fruit jam. He was shaping the oven liner on an armature of dried twigs when there came the whine of a boat's engine running at low speed.

He went to the door and saw an Avernian craft nuzzling up to his landing stage, with Felleth standing at its prow. Three other boats were wheeling across the smooth grey waters, passing the island on their way south. Snook walked down to meet Felleth, and saw that the Avernian seemed to be holding a green-and-white object in one hand. He stared hard at Felleth, projecting the customary greeting and received fleeting image of the eternal running wave.

"I was hoping you would come," he said as the Avernian stepped on to the aged planks of the landing stage. "Is there good news?"

"I think that is how you would describe it," Felleth said. With a year of practise behind him he could speak with some fluency, although his voice remained low and reedy.

"You've found another planet."

"Yes." Felleth's mouth rippled with an expression Snook had not seen before and could not interpret. "Although we had some assistance."

Snook shook his head. "I don't understand you, Felleth."

"Perhaps this will make things clear."

Felleth brought the object he was holding into clear view and Snook saw, with a lurch of his heart, that it was a green bottle which—had he been on Earth—he would instantly have identified as containing gin. Attached to it, in place of a label, was a piece of paper covered with handwriting. Felleth offered the bottle to Snook, and he took it with trembling hands. It was full of clear liquid.

"Felleth," he said in a faint voice, "what is this?"

"I do not know," Felleth replied. "The message is written in English, or another human language, and therefore I cannot read it. I presume it is intended for you."

"But . . ." Snook gazed at Felleth in perplexity for a moment, then directed his attention to the closely written message. He read:

"Dear Gil, this is yet another of my famous long shots—but you know I'm prepared to try anything in the cause of science. We have discovered two more anti-neutrino planets, one inside Pluto and one inside Uranus, and they are massive enough to modify the orbit of Thornton's Planet considerably. Avernus is going to have some very high tides in 2091—but, with proper precautions, there should be no loss of life. I have put all the relevant information into diagram form, which Felleth should be able to decipher, and it is going into a buoy which is fitted with a radio beacon. I know the Avernians do not need to use electro-magnetic phenomena for communications, but I am hoping they will detect the buoy by some means—if we get it through to Avernus safely. We have made a lot of progress in nuclear physics and in inter-universal physics in the past year, and are now in a good position to attempt a unilateral transfer on a modest scale. I am writing this on a ship in the Arabian Sea, which is as near to you as I can get on the circle of emergence, and am almost certain we can hold station with the northern top dead centre long enough to effect the transfer. If you are reading this, you will know that the experiment has been successful, and I hereby order you to celebrate by drinking the contents of the bottle. You may be interested to hear that we all got out of Barandi safely, just before there was a full-scale workers' revolution in which Ogilvie and Freeborn disappeared. Prudence has gone back to her job with UNESCO, but I know she would want me to send you her regards. Des   G 50

Quig is working with me full time, and he sends his regards as well. You may also be interested to hear that I am now married—to a lovely girl called Jody, who talks a lot but keeps me from getting too puffed up with all the publicity I get these days. There is a tremendous amount of interest in the whole concept of inter-universal transfer, and a lot of research money is going into it. There is even talk of a full-scale, manned scientific expedition to Avernus some year, and if I'm not eclipsed in the field I'll have to consider going on it —coward though I am. I don't want to promise too much, Gil, but if you get this bottle safely, make a candle-holder out of it. And put the candle in your window. Yours. Boyce."

Snook finished reading and raised his eyes to Felleth, whose slight figure was outlined on a backdrop of misty islands. He opened his mouth to say what he had read, then remembered that the Avernian would have absorbed the information directly from his mind. They looked at each other in silence, while an ocean breeze whispered past them on its journey around the world.

"It looks as though the future could be different to what I expected," Snook said.

"The present has changed as well," Felleth replied. "If you would like to live among the People, and to travel among the larger islands, it can be arranged. I can take you to my home now."

"I would like that, but I don't want to leave this island until tomorrow." Snook hefted the gin bottle. "I've got an old friend to keep me company tonight."

He said goodbye to Felleth and began walking back to his solitary house, picking his way with care on the steep and stony path.